TEACHING
& PREACHING
GOD'S WORD

CHARLIE H. CAMPBELL

"I hate the devil worse and worse every day, and I have vowed, if it be possible, by preaching the Word of God, to seek to shake the very pillars of his kingdom."

– CHARLES HADDON SPURGEON

TEACHING & PREACHING GOD'S WORD

The words of Charles Spurgeon on the previous page were taken from his sermon "An Antidote To Satan's Devices" delivered in 1858.

*Dedicated with love and thankfulness
to all the people God has called, is calling,
and will call to "Preach the Word!"*

ACKNOWLEDGMENTS

Many men have had a part in shaping the thoughts in this book, too many to list here. But chief among them are: Charles Spurgeon, G. Campbell Morgan, Martyn Lloyd-Jones, F. B. Myer, Richard Baxter, Ray Stedman, Warren Wiersbe, Brian Brodersen, Greg Laurie, Chuck Smith, Alistair Begg, John MacArthur, Richard Mayhue, Haddon Robinson, John Stott, Bryan Chapell and Al Mohler. I have benefitted much by their articles and books on the topic of preaching and their godly examples outside the pulpit.

I am also so grateful for my wife Anastasia and our five children—Selah, Addison, Caden, Emerie and Ryland. It was a blessing to have their love, support, prayers, and encouragement as I wrote these pages.

My deepest thanks go to my great God and Savior, Jesus Christ. It is He who saved me and continues to sustain me with His manifold grace. What a blessing it is to know Him and make Him known. He is the One I live for, write for, and am so blessed to serve.

CONTENTS

1. Cultivate a deep, personal, love relationship with the Lord.
2. Walk in holiness.
3. Love the people you preach to.
4. Run to the throne of grace often.
5. Rely on the power of the Holy Spirit.
6. Work hard at preaching and teaching.

7. Handle God's Word with reverence and care.
8. Diligently study the Word of God.
9. Study as early in the week as possible for an upcoming message.
10. Saturate your teaching with the Word of God.
11. Consider teaching verse-by-verse through whole books of the Bible rather than topically.
12. Don't assume your listeners know the Bible better than they do.
13. As you study and prepare, ask the six big questions.
14. Consider walking through these suggested steps when preparing a sermon.
15. Make sure the verses you look at (or cite) actually support the point you are making when they are properly interpreted in their own context.
16. Point people to Jesus.
17. Know there are typically at least five types of people in the average gathering.
18. When you are preparing your sermon, be sure to consult with other translations of the Bible.
19. Deal with the difficulties in the passage you are teaching.
20. Evaluate your conclusions in reliable sources.
21. Don't just tell your listeners *what* a passage means; show them *why* it means that.
22. Consider these seven steps as a possible framework for the delivery of your sermon.
23. Preach a big God.
24. Try to emphasize what *God* has done for the people not what *people* have done for God.
25. Be accurate with statistics.
26. Be accurate with stories.
27. Avoid alliterating your points.
28. Don't take your listeners on seemingly endless page flipping tours through the Bible.

29. Remember that where the Scriptures are silent, speculation is not necessary.
30. Be careful with how often you refer to the Greek and Hebrew.

31. Make your introductions interesting, short and clear.
32. Prepare your introduction at the end of your studying.

33. Use illustrations wisely.
34. Don't repeatedly use your favorite illustrations.
35. Use illustrations that actually serve a real purpose.
36. Don't betray someone's confidence for the sake of an illustration.
37. Avoid illustrations in which you end up being the hero.
38. Use Biblical illustrations whenever possible.

39. Exhort those you are teaching to apply the Word to their own situation and to act.
40. Do not always keep the application for the end of the message.
41. Regularly include instruction, reminders and exhortation on the Holy Spirit.

42. Finish your teaching with a strong conclusion.

43. Sleep well the night before you teach.

44. Be mindful that you preach in the sight of God.
45. Preach that God may be glorified.
46. Keep your comments brief when you step up to the pulpit.
47. Don't feel it necessary, as you begin your teaching, to always review your previous message.
48. Preach the Word with confidence and authority.
49. Speak directly to the people you are teaching, not neglecting to use the word "You."
50. Preach with passion.
51. Preach in the present tense.
52. Aim to speak clear enough so as to not be misunderstood.
53. Preach apologetically; contend for the faith.
54. Speak to the current issues of the day.
55. Preach the gospel and keep it Biblical.
56. Speak to persuade.
57. Help your listeners understand *why* God requires a particular action.
58. Restate the important stuff.
59. Honor your spouse and family in the pulpit.
60. Use humor wisely.
61. Be careful about teaching too long.

62. When teaching, try to maintain consistent eye contact with your listeners.
63. Avoid distracting body language in the pulpit.

64. Don't judge yourself by men's praise or lack of it.
65. Find someone who will offer suggestions and constructive criticism.
66. Remember your preaching continues after you've stepped down from the pulpit.
67. Be patient as God's Word germinates.

68. Spend time with other teachers.
69. Expose yourself to great preaching.
70. Try to avoid picking up the mannerisms and sayings of popular teachers. Be yourself.
71. Remember that success in preaching is pleasing God not reaching large numbers.
72. Realize you'll probably never feel like you have arrived as a teacher and if you do, it's probably time to step down.
73. Protect your relationship with the Lord.

74. As finances permit, invest in a good library.
75. Take advantage of Bible study software.
76. Record your teachings.
77. If you use PowerPoint or Keynote, use it wisely.
78. Set up a good filing system for illustrations and other interesting information.

WHY I WROTE THIS BOOK

I don't know of any greater blessing this side of Heaven than for a man to stand up week after week with God's Word in his hands and God's Spirit in his heart to speak forth God's truth into the lives of God's people. What a blessing to dig deeply into His Word and then to take those discoveries, those mined treasures, up to the pulpit to be used by the Creator of the universe to communicate them to people!

For the past twenty years, God has blessed me with this wonderful privilege. It is something I enjoy immensely. But of course—and I'm sure I'll get a hearty amen here from people who do it regularly—it is no easy task. Some preachers make it look easy, but for those of you who've done it, you know better. Teaching God's Word is a challenging ministry in a variety of ways.

Knowing that is the case, every year dozens of people who are either feeling called to teach God's Word or who are new to the task of teaching, ask me this question:

What advice or counsel would you give someone like me when it comes to sermon preparation and teaching?

They're not asking this question because they consider me a great preacher. I'm sure they don't. I don't! I think they're just eager to talk to someone who has been teaching longer than them with the hope of receiving some helpful advice and encouragement.

I love hearing this question for a couple reasons. First, it blesses me to see that God is raising up fresh laborers to fulfill the great commission (Matt. 28:19). Every generation needs a new wave of teachers to fill the ranks of those who have gone to Heaven, moved on to other ministries, or had their ministry shipwrecked for one reason or another. There is also the need for teachers who can take God's Word into areas where there is a lack of good preaching. Hearing the question above reminds me that God *is* raising up people. And we can praise Him for that.

Second, I love the humility it takes to ask this question. Pride, a sinister enemy of better preaching, whispers, "Don't ask for help. You're great already!" It takes humility to ask for advice and counsel. The person who looks for advice or encouragement with preaching realizes he hasn't arrived as a teacher. He understands he has room to grow and improve—as we all do. God loves this kind of humility. "God is opposed to the proud, but gives grace to the humble" (James 4:6).

So, I love to talk to people about preaching, not only to pass along some things I've learned and thought deeply about over the years, but because I usually end up receiving something from the other person as well. "Iron sharpens iron, so one man sharpens another" (Prov. 27:17). Unfortunately, we're usually only able to talk for a few minutes before someone else walks up with another question, a cell phone rings, lunch is over, etc. The persistency of this question is one of the reasons I decided to write this book.

To be honest though, I didn't jump into writing this book without some serious trepidation. What man in his right mind sets out to write a book on preaching? Who am I to share my thoughts, ideas, and advice on preaching with other pastors and teachers? I mean I can understand why Charles Spurgeon, Warren Wiersbe, Martyn Lloyd-Jones, Alistair Begg and others decided to write books on the topic, but *me*? Don't I know that most pastors and teachers are too busy preparing sermons and preaching to read a book about preparing sermons and preaching?

Those are the kinds of questions that have probably killed ten thousand books on this topic before they ever got off the ground. Those nagging questions followed me around like a pack of wild dogs for months as I prayerfully contemplated writing this book. But alas! What is a man to do who has a burden to write about these things? I decided to put my hand to the plow, start writing and leave God to deal with the dogs. The book you hold in your hands is the result.

In the pages to follow you'll find dozens of concise suggestions, ideas, exhortations, and words of encouragement on sermon preparation and preaching.

Each chapter stands alone. That is to say, the chapters are independent of one another. You don't have to grasp a concept in an earlier chapter to understand something in a latter one. This means you can read the book in any order you'd like. In fact, when I first penned the different chapters, I wrote them in a completely random order as certain topics came to mind. And I almost left them in the book that way. It was only near the book's completion when I was laying out the table of contents that I decided to arrange the chapters under certain headings. I did this for what I hope will be your benefit, but even now as I type this, I'm wondering whether the book might be more fun to read if each chapter was completely unrelated to the chapter before and after it. Be that as it may, I encourage you to read the whole book, but feel free to use the table of contents and find the chapters you think might be most beneficial to you and read those chapters first.

I purposely kept the chapters concise with the hope that doing so would make it easier for busy people to digest the book's contents in bite size chunks.

In any case dear friend, I pray that God will see fit to use this book to aid you as you sojourn with His people and feed them on their way to Heaven.

Charlie Campbell
March 6, 2013
Carlsbad, California

HAVE YOU BEEN GIFTED AND CALLED TO TEACH?

All Christians should be looking for opportunities to teach people the Scriptures and make disciples (Deut. 6:7, Matt. 28:19–20). Writing to the believers in Colossae, the apostle Paul said:

> Let the word of Christ richly dwell within you, with all wisdom *teaching* and admonishing one another with psalms and hymns and spiritual songs, singing with thankfulness in your hearts to God (Col. 3:16).

So, all believers are to be teachers in some sense, ministering the Word of God to "one another" within the body of Christ, our families, our sphere of influence, etc. But God has blessed

17

the church with certain individuals He has specifically *gifted* to be teachers. The Bible says:

> And He Himself gave some to be apostles, some prophets, some evangelists, and some pastors and *teachers*, for the equipping of the saints for the work of ministry, for the edifying of the body of Christ (Eph. 4:11–12 NKJV).

There are certain people God has gifted and called to equip the saints (the redeemed) for the work of ministry. They are often the pastors, Sunday school teachers, home fellowship leaders, women's ministry leaders, etc. within the church.

A question often on the minds of people who think they may be called to be one of these teachers is:

How can a person discern whether or not he[1] has been appointed (called by God) to this kind of teaching ministry?

Maybe you've asked that question.

When a person asks me this question, I like to ask him three questions in order to help him discover the direction God may be leading him. I think his answers to these questions are often very revealing as to whether or not God is calling him to a teaching role. Here are the questions I ask:

Things to ask
- Do you have a strong *desire* to teach?
- Do you sense that you are *gifted* at teaching?
- When you teach, are God's people giving you

---

[1] I refer to teachers of God's Word throughout this book with masculine pronouns. By doing so, I do not mean to diminish the important role women have in the body of Christ teaching women and children (Titus 2:3–4). I hope many women who teach the Bible are able to find much encouragement in this book.

encouraging feedback afterwards? (Do God's people seem to be genuinely thankful and blessed when you teach them?)

Here's why I ask those specific questions.

1. Do you have a strong desire to teach?

One of the ways God directs us into His will for our lives is by planting His desires in our hearts. The Psalmist said, "Delight yourself in the LORD; and He will give you the *desires* of your heart" (Ps. 37:4). The Bible says that God "works in you both *to will* and to do for His good pleasure" (Phil. 2:13 NKJV).

If you have a desire to teach God's Word to others—if you have a burden for the well-being of God's people—if your heart longs to open up God's Word and counsel others with its truths—if you feel you *must* teach, those are good indications God is leading you to teach.

Jeremiah said, "His word was in my heart like a burning fire shut up in my bones; I was weary of holding it back, and I could not" (Jer. 20:9 NKJV). In other words, Jeremiah said, "I had to speak His Word. I couldn't remain silent!" what I need

If you have that kind of desire, it's fairly safe to assume that to do in my life God planted it in your heart. The natural man does not have desires like that. The carnal believer doesn't have desires like that. It's usually the believer who is being led by the Holy Spirit to teach who has desires like that. Whatever the case, if you have a desire to teach, it's time to start praying and asking the Lord for wisdom regarding what to do with that desire.

2. Do you sense that you are gifted at teaching?

I believe when God calls a person to teach, God also bestows the gift of teaching. The apostle Peter wrote:

> As each one has *received* a gift, *minister it* to one another, as good stewards of the manifold grace of God. If anyone speaks, let him speak as the oracles of God (1 Pet. 4:10–11 NKJV)

God glorifying ministry takes place when people use their God-given gifts to bless others. The truest test that a person has been called to teach will be that he will be *able* to teach. Paul said:

> And the things that you have heard from me among many witnesses, commit these to faithful men who will be *able to teach* others also (2 Tim. 2:2 NKJV).

Paul continued in the same chapter:

> And a servant of the Lord must not quarrel but be gentle to all, *able to teach*, patient, in humility correcting those who are in opposition (2 Tim. 2:24–25a NKJV).

And again to Timothy, Paul wrote:

> An overseer, then, must be above reproach, the husband of one wife, temperate, prudent, respectable, hospitable, *able to teach* (1 Tim. 3:2).

How do we determine if someone is "able to teach?" Quite simply, when a person is able to teach, people will leave his teachings *understanding* what the Word of God means and how to apply it to their life. This doesn't mean that a person who is called to teach will be an exceptional teacher the first or second year he is at it, but there should be an ability to teach that is *progressing* (1 Tim. 4:13–15).

3. When you teach, are God's people giving you *encouraging* feedback afterwards?

I ask this because when a person is gifted at teaching, God's people, at least some of them, will rally around and support a good teacher with thankfulness and encouraging feedback. They know what a gift (Eph. 4:11) a good teacher is to a fellowship of believers and they don't want him to stop or prematurely abandon his post.

If you are already teaching somewhere but questioning whether or not you are really *called* to a teaching ministry, you might consider what's happening at the venue you teach at. You may not be called to teach if:

- Newcomers only show up a couple of times and then mysteriously stop coming[2]
- No one is giving you positive feedback after you teach
- No one is encouraging you to keep teaching

If these things continually describe what's happening when you teach, I encourage you to be in conversation with godly friends and in prayer to God about whether or not God has really called you to a teaching ministry. Perhaps He has, but things are just getting off to a slow start. But, the other possibility is that God has not called you to a teaching ministry and

---

[2] Of course, there are lots of reasons why newcomers don't stick around. They may be from out of town. They may not like the worship, the décor of the church, the uncomfortable seats, the temperature of the venue, etc. But people will tolerate quite a few shortcomings if the teaching is good.

has something else for you to do. There are lots of other places to serve in the church today besides in a teaching role.

If you believe God has called you to teach, please read on.

THE PREACHER'S HEART & CHARACTER

1. Cultivate a deep, personal, love relationship with the Lord.

> *"Great preaching begins with a great relationship with God. It is impossible for a preacher to compensate for a relationship that has gone cold, for the 'mouth speaks from the overflow of the heart.'"[3] –J. Kent Edwards*

The highest priority for any person who wants to teach God's Word to His people is knowing and loving God personally, intimately, deeply. God says:

---

[3] J. Kent Edwards, *Deep Preaching*, 44.

Let not a wise man boast of his wisdom, and let not the mighty man boast of his might, let not a rich man boast of his riches; but let him who boasts boast of this, that he *understands* and *knows* Me, that I am the LORD who exercises lovingkindness, justice, and righteousness on earth; for I delight in these things (Jer. 9:23b–24).

Wisdom in teaching is important, as is strength—preaching requires hard work. But nothing is as important as knowing and loving God (Jn. 17:3; Mk. 12:28–30). The apostle Paul said:

I count all things to be loss in view of the surpassing value of *knowing* Christ Jesus my Lord, for whom I have suffered the loss of all things, and count them but rubbish so that I may gain Christ (Phil. 3:8).

Paul considered everything that men count valuable to be worthless in comparison with knowing Jesus. That's how paramount knowing the Lord was to Paul. And it should be for us also.

Before you are a preacher, teacher, or servant in any capacity *for* the King, you are a son—an adopted son—*of* the King (Gal. 4:5; Eph. 1:5).[4] He adopted you! He loves you. He's not concerned first and foremost about your ministry or your service. He's interested in *you*. He wants to have a relationship with you. He wants to meet with you often and dine with you (Rev. 3:20). He wants to hear what's on your heart (Prov. 15:8; 1 Pet. 5:7). And, as your loving Father, He wants to encourage you, teach you and lead you. He made you for this very reason,

---

[4] I'm assuming all the readers of this book have been forgiven of their sins, born again, and reconciled to God.

so that you could know and enjoy Him now and throughout eternity (Jn. 17:3).

So, before I give you any practical how-to advice on teaching, I exhort you fellow brother: Know your Father well! Spend time daily meditating in the Scriptures—thinking them over, dwelling on them, praying to God about them with thanksgiving, praise, and a determination to obey. Not for sermon preparation. That can happen later in the day. I'm talking about in your own regular quiet time with the Lord. During that time in the Scriptures, you're not asking God, "What do You want me to say to the *congregation*?" You're asking God, "What do You want to teach *me*?" Because as a son, your quiet time with your Father is *not preparation* for the next sermon you're preaching, it's your time to bless God and enjoy Him for your own benefit, your own edification.

Now, this isn't to say that knowing God deeply won't affect your sermons. It certainly will. People who know God well make the best teachers. Think about it. Would you rather listen to a lecture about President Ronald Reagan by someone who has read a couple of books about him or by a person who actually knew him personally, someone who lived with him, ate with him and was even an adopted son?[5] I don't know about you, but I'd rather listen to the person who knew "Ronnie" personally.

I think the same is true with God's people who are hungry to know the Lord. They want to hear from someone who knows God deeply and personally—someone whose relationship with the Lord is more than academic. It's genuine. It's deep. It's rich. It's personal. And it shows up when they are in the pulpit.

---

[5] Michael Reagan is the adopted son of the late Ronald Reagan. He speaks frequently regarding his father.

God's people are attracted to that kind of teacher. And for the preacher who regularly draws near to God and knows Him in that manner, preaching is not drudgery; it's a joy. He's not telling people about a remote deity; he's telling people about his "Abba! Father!" (Rom. 8:15). He's able to explain to the congregation what the Scriptures teach (because he's studied the passage adequately) but he's also able to share out of the overflow of what he's gleaned through the years during his own times of meditating on the Word (Matt. 13:52). He's able to share from his own deep treasure chest what God has revealed to him in his quiet time in the Word. And God's people soak that up and to much benefit.

So, my friend, press into the Lord! Know Him well.

2.   Walk in holiness.

"But like the Holy One who called you, be holy
yourselves also in all your behavior."
(1 Pet. 1:15)

If knowing and loving God is of supreme importance in the life of the preacher,[6] holiness is right there near the top of the list. I agree with E. M. Bounds who said:

It is not great talents or great learning or great preachers that God needs, but men great in *holiness*, great in faith, great in love, great in fidelity, great for God—men always preaching by *holy* sermons in the pulpit, by *holy* lives out of it. These can mold a generation for God.[7]

---

[6] See chapter one.

[7] E. M. Bounds, *Power through Prayer*, 14.

These men—"men great in holiness"—can mold a generation for God. If you are not a man of God, it will be difficult to stand before the people of God to preach the Word of God. Robert Murray M'Cheyne, the influential Scottish preacher of the nineteenth century, said: "My people's greatest need is my personal holiness."[8] He's right. There is no faster way to weaken or shipwreck your teaching ministry than to compromise with sin. Why is sin so detrimental to a preacher's ability to teach? Sin:

- Grieves the Holy Spirit (Eph. 4:30)
- Brings about feelings of shame (Rom. 6:21)
- Robs you of the joy of your salvation (Ps. 51:12)
- Obscures fellowship with the Lord (1 Jn. 1:7)
- Brings sorrow (Prov. 22:8; Ps. 118:15a)
- Multiplies your problems (Prov. 11:27)
- Leads to more sin (Rom. 6:19)
- Dishonors God (1 Cor. 6:19–20)
- Will hinder your prayer life (1 Pet. 3:7, 12)
- Will make your life spiritually powerless (1 Cor. 9:27)
- Causes good things from God to be withheld (Jer. 5:25)
- Inhibits spiritual growth (1 Cor. 3:1)
- Brings chastisement from the Lord (Heb. 12:5–7)
- Prevents you being a fit vessel for the Lord to use (2 Tim. 2:21)
- Pollutes Christian fellowship (1 Cor. 10:21)
- Prevents participating properly in the Lord's Supper (1 Cor. 11:28–29)
- Brings about corruption (Rom. 6:21; Gal. 6:7–8)
- Can endanger your physical life and health (1 Cor. 11:30; 1 Jn. 5:16)[9]

---

[8] Mcheyne.info/quotes.php

[9] Many of these were adapted from *The MacArthur New Testament Commentary*, Romans 7:14–25, 380.

No wonder Peter says to "be holy...in all your behavior" (1 Pet. 1:15). Sin's price tag is more than you want to pay.

So friend, prioritize holiness. Be careful with what you allow into your home and your mind. Be careful with the company you keep. Put Internet protection or accountability software on your computers, your tablet, your cell phone. Pray for a victorious, holy life. Pray for sanctification. Pray that God will deliver you from the snares the devil will set for you. Be a vessel of honor, a vessel God can continue to find useful. Paul said:

> Therefore, if *anyone cleanses himself* from these things, he will be a vessel for honor, sanctified, *useful to the Master,* prepared for every good work. Now flee from youthful lusts and pursue righteousness, faith, love and peace, with those who call on the Lord from a pure heart (2 Tim. 2:21–22).

Do you want to be useful to the Master? Walk in holiness.

3.   Love the people you preach to.

"We know that we have passed out of death into life, because we love the brethren." (1 Jn. 3:14)

When George Pentecost finished a discourse in the city of Edinburgh, Horatius Bonar put his hand upon his shoulder and said, "You love to preach to men, don't you?" and Dr. Pentecost answered, "Yes." Then Mr. Bonar said, "Do you love the men you preach to?"[10] To love to preach is one thing, to love those to whom you preach is quite another.

---

[10] *Illustrations of Bible Truths*, compiled by Ruth Peters, QuickVerse.

Some teachers end up loving reading, studying, teaching, and ministry more than they love the people. That should not be the case.

> If I speak with the tongues of men and of angels, but do not have love, I have become a noisy gong or a clanging cymbal. And if I have the gift of prophecy [teaching], and know all mysteries and all knowledge; and if I have all faith, so as to remove mountains, but do not have love, I am nothing (1 Cor. 13:1–2).

The primary motivation to read, study and prepare sermons should be our love for God and for people. Our love for people leads us to want the very best for them. And we believe that teaching them God's Word will lead them into fuller lives—lives that will glorify Christ and bring them into God's very best. So, *that* is why we read, study and prepare sermons. God forbid we get our priorities out of order and have more love for learning and sermon development than the Savior and the saints the sermons are for! I agree with Wallace Benn who says:

> My concern is that preachers have little pastoral contact with ordinary people except in emergencies...Indeed, we must honestly admit that some preachers appear not to like people much, withdrawing from contact with them and sometimes justifying it by saying they believe in the priority of preaching...I believe passionately in the priority of preaching, but this must not be used to distance us from involvement with people.[11]

---

[11] Wallace Benn, "Preaching with a Pastor's Heart: Richard Baxter's *The Reformed Pastor*," in *Preach the Word: Essays on Expository Preaching in Honor of R. Kent Hughes*, 134.

You who are called by God to teach His Word, I encourage you to:

- Cultivate relationships with the people you teach
- Talk to them after the teaching
- Get to know them
- Become a part of their lives
- Find out how they are doing
- Visit them in the hospital
- Meet with them for lunch
- Listen to their struggles
- Pray for them while you're with them[12]

Spending time with the sheep will not only benefit them, it will benefit your preaching. It is much easier to know your listeners' questions, needs, struggles and challenges when you know your flock.

4. Run to the throne of grace often.

"How little time the average Christian spends
in prayer. We are too busy to pray, and so we are
too busy to have power. We have a great deal of
activity, but we accomplish little; many services but
few conversions; much machinery but
few results."[13] –R. A. Torrey

Preparing sermons and preaching them is no easy task. It is the foolhardy fellow who jumps into the task of studying and

---

[12] Don't just say, "I'll pray for you." Pray for them right there!

[13] Rueben Archer Torrey, *How to Obtain Fulness of Power in Christian Life and Service*, 81.

sermon building without first humbly seeking God's help. Surely, this is all work that needs God's blessing if it is going to be done well and to God's glory. The way to access the help God wants to provide is through prayer. The Scriptures are filled with encouragements to pray.

- Abraham prayed and Abimelech's life was spared and wombs were opened (Gen. 20:17)

- Moses prayed and God's judgment on Israel was stayed (Num. 14)

- Joshua prayed and the sun stood still (Josh. 10)

- Hannah prayed and her womb was opened (1 Sam. 1:11–20)

- Elijah prayed and it stopped raining for three and a half years (1 Ki. 17–18)

- Hezekiah prayed and fifteen years were added to his life (2 Ki. 20:1–6)

- Zacharias and Elizabeth prayed and John was conceived (Lk. 1:13)

- Jesus prayed for Peter that his faith would not fail and Peter led the early church (Lk. 22:32)

- The church prayed for boldness in the face of the Sanhedrin's threats and the Holy Spirit empowered them to "speak the word of God with boldness" (Acts 4:31)

- The church prayed and Peter was released from prison (Acts 12:5)

These are encouraging reminders that indeed, "The effective, fervent prayer of a righteous man avails much" (James 5:16 NKJV). So, pray for your study time. Pray for the flock. Pray for yourself. Pray for the teaching. "Let us come boldly to the throne of grace, that we may obtain mercy and find grace to help in time of need" (Heb. 4:16 NKJV).

5. Rely on the power of the Holy Spirit.

"And they were all filled with the Holy Spirit, and began to speak the Word of God with boldness." (Acts 4:31)

Richard Baxter, the beloved Puritan pastor and theologian of the seventeenth century, said:

> Our work requireth greater skill, and especially greater life and zeal than any of us bring to it. It is no small matter to stand up in the face of a congregation, and to deliver a message of salvation or damnation, as from the living God, in the name of the Redeemer. It is no easy matter to speak so plainly, that the most ignorant may understand us; and so seriously that the deadest hearts may feel us; and so convincingly, that the contradicting cavillers[14] may be silenced.[15]

True indeed. Thankfully, God has not asked you to prepare sermons or stand before His people in your own strength (Eph.

---

[14] Those who make petty or unnecessary objections.
[15] Richard Baxter, *The Reformed Pastor*, 117.

6:10). The Bible says that the person who serves in any capacity should do so in the power God supplies. 1 Peter 4:11 says:

> Whoever speaks, let him speak, as it were, the utterances of God; whoever serves, *let him do so as by the strength which God supplies*; so that in all things God may be glorified through Jesus Christ, to whom belongs the glory and dominion forever and ever. Amen.

How can you teach in "the strength which God supplies"? Well, seeing that the strength is something that God supplies, you don't have to manufacture it on your own. The way to access this strength is through prayer (Luke 21:36).

Before I teach, I ask God to fill me with the power of His Holy Spirit. I tell Him I want to minister in the strength which He supplies (Zech. 4:6). I confess to Him that apart from Him, I can do nothing (Jn. 15:5). I pray for His help. I pray for insight. I pray for humility, boldness, love, a good memory of what I've studied and clear speech to communicate what He would have me to say. I pray that His people would receive "edification and exhortation and consolation" (1 Cor. 14:3). I pray that the lost would be saved. I thank Him for the privilege of standing before His people to teach them.

Then, I trust the Lord. I remember that He has promised to never leave us as we go out to teach and make disciples (Matt. 28:18–20). And then, I walk up to the pulpit and trust that God is going to bless the going forth of His Word (Isa. 55:10–11).

Countless times I have sensed my weakness being turned into strength as a result of God hearing my prayer and answering according to His will.

Now, having the power of the Holy Spirit doesn't mean that those who step up to the pulpit can slack off in preparation. And that brings me to my next point.

6. Work hard at preaching and teaching.

"It is our duty and our privilege to exhaust our lives for Jesus. We are not to be living specimens of men in fine preservation, but living sacrifices, whose lot is to be consumed."[16] –Charles Spurgeon

The story is told of a pastor who never prepared during the week and on Sunday morning he would sit on the stage while the church was singing, desperately praying, "Lord, give Your message, Lord give me Your message." One Sunday, as he cried out to God for His message, he heard the Lord say, "Ralph, here's My message. You're lazy!" Ouch.

Resist the temptation to be lazy when it comes to studying, preparing sermons and teaching. The Bible says, "Let the elders who rule well be considered worthy of double honor, especially those who *work hard* at preaching and teaching" (1 Tim. 5:17). Notice that. We who teach God's Word should be hard workers. And for good reason! God is worthy of our wholehearted efforts. We are servants working for the most gracious, benevolent Master imaginable—our Heavenly Father who delivered us from the kingdom of darkness. How could we repay Him with a slack hand at the work He's appointed us to? Well, we won't! We will gladly work hard for Him.

Charles Spurgeon often worked eighteen hours a day. David Livingstone, the famous missionary to Africa, once asked him, "How do you manage to do two men's work in a

---

[16] Charles Spurgeon, *Lectures to My Students*, 156–157.

single day?" Spurgeon replied, "You have forgotten there are two of us."[17] Two of us—the preacher and the Lord. 1 Corinthians 3:9 says, "We are God's fellow workers." You are not alone in your ministry. Paul said, "I labor, striving according to His power, which mightily works within me" (Col. 1:29).

If you approach your calling as a teacher with laziness and think, "Well, I will just trust that the Holy Spirit will help me," you're actually straying from what the Bible says will mark the life of honorable teachers—hard work. The most fruitful preaching is the result of the Holy Spirit working through men who "work hard" (cf. 1 Cor. 15:10; Col. 1:29).

Some have used Matthew 10:19–20 to justify their "I'll just trust the Lord to speak through me" attitude when it comes to sermon preparation. Here in this passage, Jesus said:

> Do not worry about how or what you should speak. For it will be given to you in that hour what you should speak; for it is not you who speak, but the Spirit of your Father who speaks in you (Matt. 10:19b–20 NKJV).

Was Jesus giving us assurance here that we can neglect studying and just trust Him when it's time to teach? No. Let's look at the passage in its context. Let's start back in verse sixteen. Jesus said to His disciples:

> Behold, I send you out as sheep in the midst of wolves. Therefore be wise as serpents and harmless as doves. But beware of men, for they will deliver you up to councils and scourge you in their synagogues. You will be brought before governors and kings for My sake, as a testimony to them

---

[17] Eric W. Hayden, "Did You Know?" *Christian History Magazine*, Issue 29, 1991, 2–3.

and to the Gentiles. But when they deliver you up, do not worry about how or what you should speak. For it will be given to you in that hour what you should speak; for it is not you who speak, but the Spirit of your Father who speaks in you (Matt. 10:16–20 NKJV).

Notice the context. Jesus said, "But when they deliver you up." Who would deliver the disciples up? Wolves, enemies of the gospel. Why would the disciples be delivered up? To be scourged (v. 17) and brought before councils (courts) and governors and kings. Jesus was talking about law courts, *not the church*, home fellowships, etc.

Being dragged off to be scourged and to stand before governors, would not allow the disciples time to prepare their defense. It would be *then* that the Holy Spirit would give them the necessary words and even the boldness to share their testimonies (v. 18).

Jesus' words were not intended to comfort the person who is too lazy or proud to work hard preparing for a teaching. If a man thinks he's just going to wing it when he steps up to the pulpit and trust the Holy Spirit, he will discover very quickly that is not how the Lord often works.

The Bible is clear. Work hard (1 Tim. 5:17) at preaching and teaching and rely on the power of the Holy Spirit as you do.

THE PREPARATION
OF THE SERMON

7. Handle God's Word with reverence and care.

"Let him who has My word speak My word faithfully." (Jer. 23:28 ESV)

When you sit down to open the Bible and prepare a sermon, realize what it is you are opening. The book that lies before you is the holy, God-breathed revelation bestowed upon humanity from the Creator of the universe. It is *God's* Word, not ours. We should dread the thought of standing before God's people and maligning it, misinterpreting it, mishandling it, or misapplying it in any way, even unintentionally.

You need to be careful to deliver God's Word to God's people intact, without twisting the text or distorting its meaning in any way.

> Be diligent to present yourself *approved* to God, a worker who does not need to be ashamed, *rightly* dividing the word of truth (2 Timothy 2:15 NKJV).

To have God's approval of your teaching, you must rightly divide the Word. In other words, you must handle it correctly. To do this, you must handle God's Word with reverence and be careful with your interpretations.[18]

8. Diligently study the Word of God.

"He was mighty in the Scriptures."
(Acts 18:24)

If you want to teach God's Word to others, you must determine to become a serious *student* of the Scriptures. Do not be content in just reading the Bible. That may suffice for the average believer, but if you are going to teach God's Word accurately, you must study the Bible. I love what Luke writes about Apollos in the Book of Acts:

---

[18] This book deals almost exclusively with preaching the Word (*homiletics*). For more on rightly dividing the Word (*hermeneutics*), see the link "Hermeneutics" at AlwaysBeReady.com. There I discuss rules and guidelines to aid the teacher in properly interpreting the Scriptures.

Now a Jew named Apollos, an Alexandrian by birth, an eloquent man, came to Ephesus; and he was *mighty in the Scriptures* (Acts 18:24).

Luke says Apollos was "mighty in the Scriptures." He had a great grasp on the Scriptures. That's something every teacher of the Scriptures should desire to have.

Do you desire that? How does one develop a great grasp on the Scriptures? Well, we can follow Ezra's lead:

For Ezra had *set his heart* to study the law of the LORD, and to practice it, and to teach His statutes and ordinances in Israel (Ezra 7:10).

Ezra made a decision: *'I am going to study the Word of God!'* That's what we need to do.

The well-known pastor and teacher, John MacArthur relates the time when:

A young man said to me, "What is the real key to great preaching?" And he was kind of starry-eyed and I'm sure he expected some spiritual esoteric answer, 'Well, it's the ability to keep your rear end in the chair till you understand the text.' Boy, he was shocked. Yeah, that's the real key. What separates great preaching from poor preaching is whether you know what you're talking about or not.[19]

Studying until you really understand the text is vitally important to good preaching. It's not always easy. Sometimes it can be long, time-consuming work.

---

[19] Excerpted from a transcript of a sermon titled "The Inspiration of the Scriptures" by John MacArthur. http://www.gty.org/resources/Print/Sermons/90–156.

I once heard the story of a world famous violin player. Someone asked her how she got so good at playing. Her answer? *"Planned neglect."* Planned neglect? That was an odd answer. The person questioned her on this. Then she explained:

> There were many things that used to demand my time. When I went to my room after breakfast, I made my bed, straightened the room, dusted, and did whatever seemed necessary. When I finished my work, I turned to my violin practice. That system prevented me from accomplishing what I should on the violin. So I reversed things. I deliberately planned to neglect everything else until my practice period was complete. And that program of planned neglect is the secret of my success.[20]

That inspires me. Planned neglect!

- Knowing the importance and value of true, Biblical, expository preaching

- Knowing that it is God's Word alone that He promises will not return void (Isaiah 55:11)

- Knowing that it is the "the Holy Scriptures, which are able to make [one] wise for salvation through faith which is in Christ Jesus" (2 Tim. 3:15 NKJV)

- Knowing that it is God's Word alone that "is living and powerful, and sharper than any two-edged sword, piercing even to the division of soul and spirit" (Heb. 4:12 NKJV)

---

[20] This story originally appeared in *Our Daily Bread*. http://bible.org/illustration/planned-neglect.

- Knowing it is God's Word that makes a person "complete, thoroughly equipped for every good work" (2 Tim. 3:17 NKJV)

…may I encourage you who plan on teaching God's Word to others? *Plan on neglecting some things.* That might mean you turn off your television, cancel the cable, let your subscription to *Sports Illustrated* expire, miss a round of golf, get rid of your PlayStation, check your Twitter or Facebook feeds less, etc.

Examine your weekly routine. What do you waste time doing? Could you dedicate some or all of that time to studying the Word? I bet you could if you'll purpose in your heart like Ezra to study the Word.

I'll have more to say about *how* to study later on. I'll end this chapter with a reminder from G. Campbell Morgan:

> The supreme work of the Christian minister is the work of preaching. This is a day in which one of our great perils is that of doing a thousand little things to the neglect of the one thing, which is preaching.[21]

There are a thousand little things one could get involved in. Neglect those, not the preaching. If this was an important reminder to preachers in Morgan's lifetime (1863–1945), it is even more so today with the myriad of modern distractions fighting for our attention.

---

[21] G. Campbell Morgan, *Preaching*, 12.

9. Study as early in the week as possible for an upcoming message.

"Messages mature over time...Relevant thoughts and insights can come to mind while driving the car, waiting in a line, or even in the middle of an important conversation."[22] –Stephen Olford

I always begin studying for an upcoming teaching the day after I teach the previous study. So, if I teach on Sunday, on Monday I will read through the passage of Scripture I'll be covering the next Sunday. This allows me time to start:

- Mulling over what I am going to be teaching on
- Praying for wisdom on how to teach it
- Thinking about illustrations
- Applying it to my own life, etc.

I encourage you to do likewise. The head start you give yourself by doing this will prove beneficial to you and will help you prepare a better message for those whom you are teaching.

---

[22] Stephen Olford and David Olford, *Anointed Expository Preaching*, 106.

10. Saturate your teaching with the Word of God.

"So will My word be which goes forth from My mouth; it will not return to Me empty, without accomplishing what I desire, and without succeeding in the matter for which I sent it." (Isaiah 55:11)

It seems to me that more and more men standing behind pulpits today are neglecting to heed Paul's words to Timothy to "preach the Word" (2 Tim. 4:2). Many read a verse or a paragraph or two but then launch into all kinds of other things—stories, jokes, quotes from books, video clips, and everything *but* the Word! And sadly the result is malnourished, underfed, believers who:

- Don't know the Scriptures
- Have shallow walks with the Lord
- Are easy prey for the cults, false teachers, and every other unbiblical teaching that blows through the church

What a tragedy this is in our generation!

I think some of the blame for the success of the "emerging church movement" and its liberal, even heretical theology, falls at the feet of seeker-sensitive churches. For the past few decades they have neglected to teach God's Word in any kind of in-depth expositional manner and as a result, they have raised up a generation of young people in the church who don't know the Word of God. And so when someone hands people in their congregations books like:

- *Velvet Elvis* by Rob Bell
- *The Shack* by William Young
- *Everything Must Change* by Brian McLaren

...they are not even able to spot anything unbiblical in them. When they turn on Oprah, the same thing goes. When they read Joel Osteen, same thing. It all sounds fine to them. This is heartbreaking!

What would have prevented this? Paul told Timothy, and us by implication, "I charge you therefore before God and the Lord Jesus Christ, who will judge the living and the dead at His appearing and His kingdom: *Preach the Word!*" (2 Tim. 4:1–2 NKJV). He didn't say, "Make sure you include a citation from the Word." He didn't say, "Preach *from* the Word (as though it was some sort of a launching pad for all the other stuff you want to say). Paul said, "Preach *the* Word!" Your messages should be saturated with Scripture. They should ooze Scripture.

I sat in on a Bible study—if it could be called that—a while back at a church I was visiting. The pastor started off his teaching time by showing a ten-minute clip from a movie. Then he went on to talk about how the movie clip was illustrative of the fact that Christians need times to rest. There was no opening of the Bible. I thought, "He's got a 30 minute slot to teach and he just wasted most of that time showing us a movie clip and talking about the movie?!" I wanted to stand up and say, "Bring out the Book!" (Neh. 8:1) and "Preach the Word!" (2 Tim. 4:2). I didn't. But in churches all over the world God's people are suffering under this kind of Scripturally-starved teaching week in and week out.

Oh, but how they prosper wherever His Word is clearly and consistently laid open before them. And for good reason! Listen to what God likens the Scriptures to. We're told in the Bible that the Scriptures are like:

- **Water** that washes clean (Eph. 5:26)
- **Seed** that can bring forth fruit (Mk. 4:14)
- **Milk** that nourishes us (1 Pet. 2:2)
- **Meat** (solid food) that satisfies us (Heb. 5:14)
- **Fire** that cleanses us (Jer. 23:29)
- A **hammer** that shatters us (Jer. 23:29)
- A **sword** that cuts deeply (Heb. 4:12)
- **Medicine** to keep us from the sickness of sin (Ps. 119:11)
- A **lamp** to our feet and a light to our path (Ps. 119:105)
- A **mirror** that reflects ourselves to us (James 1:23–25)
- A **tutor** that leads us to Christ (Gal. 3:24)
- A **counselor** that comforts us (Rom. 15:4)
- That which **revives** us (Ps. 119:50)
- A **forecaster** that never fails us (2 Pet. 1:19)
- That which makes us **wiser** than our enemies (Ps. 119:98)[23]

How vital, how important then God's Word is in the life of the believer!

The greatest thing that could happen in the church today would be a wholehearted return by men who occupy pulpits to expository preaching. When I say "expository preaching" I mean preaching that is committed to:

- Opening up the Word of God
- Unpacking what the Bible says
- Explaining what it means
- Illustrating the passage when necessary

---

[23] Most of these are taken from Norman Geisler, *Systematic Theology*, Vol. 1, 250–251.

- And giving clear, passionate exhortation on how it applies to the lives of believers and nonbelievers

If more pastors and Bible teachers in youth ministries, women's ministries, etc. would return to this method of preaching I believe there would be a massive revival amongst God's people.

Now, obviously we can't do much to change what other people are doing in their churches but we can resolve in our own lives and churches to do (or continue to do) the very thing the Holy Spirit spoke through Paul to Timothy: Preach the Word! And perhaps as God would bless our efforts, other pastors would see God's people thriving, our churches growing, and wonder, "What in the world is going on over there?"

Should they inquire, we will unashamedly tell them, "It's the Lord. We are just loving the people and consistently giving the people the water that washes clean (Eph. 5:26), the seed that brings forth fruit (Mk. 4:14), the milk that nourishes (1 Pet. 2:2), the meat that satisfies (Heb. 5:14), the fire that cleanses (Jer. 23:29) and the medicine that keeps us from the sickness of sin (Ps. 119:11)." And it might just inspire them to do the same.

11. Consider teaching verse-by-verse through whole books of the Bible rather than topically.

"For I have not shunned to declare to you the whole counsel of God." (Acts 20:27 NKJV)

Seeing how vital the Word is to God's people (see previous point), there are a few reasons I encourage preachers to consider teaching verse-by-verse through entire books of the

Bible, rather than teaching topically.[24] This is not to say that topical teaching is bad. There are times when I think topical messages are perfectly appropriate and even to be preferred. Topical messages:

- Can provide variety
- Can give people a better understanding of a particular subject
- Allow us to deal with major biblical themes, doctrines and ethical teachings in an in-depth way

Having said that, I do believe verse-by-verse teaching should make up the bulk of our teaching calendar. Here's why:

A. Verse-by-verse teaching will save you time.

Trying to decide upon a text and topic to teach on once or twice a week is no easy task. Most teachers find this quite difficult. There are half a dozen questions spinning around in the minds of teachers who teach topically:

- What haven't I taught on lately?
- What does the congregation need to hear?
- Didn't I just teach on something like that a few months ago?
- What's happened in the news this week that I might address?
- Who's going to be there this Sunday? ("Oh, the man that struggles with _____ is going to be visiting with a friend.

---

[24] Teaching verse-by-verse doesn't mean the teacher needs to stop and explain every verse. When I say verse-by-verse I am talking about systematically progressing through the text of a particular book and along the way helping the people to know what the passage is saying.

I better not preach about that or it will seem like I picked that topic just for him.")

For the person who teaches verse-by-verse, there is really only one question: Where did I leave off last week? Once that question is answered he can get right to studying and preparing. Seeing how busy most pastors and teachers are today, I think you can see how beneficial this would be.

B. Teaching verse-by-verse will prove more beneficial to you spiritually.

The person who teaches topically is more likely to avoid passages and topics that he may struggle with. If he struggles with a short temper, it is likely that he will avoid teaching a topical study on *anger* or verses like this one:

> Be quick to hear, slow to speak and slow to anger; for the anger of man does not achieve the righteousness of God (James 1:19b–20).

And yet, this might be the very topic and Scripture that would be most beneficial for him to teach on. Anger is an area God surely wants to work out of this man's life.

By teaching topically, the teacher has the final say as to what he'll study and teach. The person who teaches verse-by-verse, has no choice. If his last teaching ended at James 1:18, this week he's going to be reading, studying, and praying about God's will regarding anger.

C. Teaching verse-by-verse will prove more beneficial to your listeners.

One of the huge disadvantages for people who sit under topical preaching every week is that they may never hear what God's Word has to say about:

- Controversial topics (e.g., homosexuality, Hell, repentance, sin, sexual purity, giving)
- Difficult to interpret passages (e.g., the Book of Revelation)
- Deep theological truths that are so beneficial to believers (e.g., Romans 5 and its focus on justification by faith)

Pastors who avoid these issues and passages of Scripture are doing God's people a disservice.

Why do some teachers avoid these topics and scriptures? There are a variety of reasons of course. But I think it's safe to say in some cases it is a fear of offending people and perhaps losing some of their congregation.

I encourage you to not let the fear of man become a snare (Prov. 29:25) or dictate what to teach. I love what Paul told the elders in Ephesus: "For I have not shunned to declare to you the *whole* counsel of God" (Acts 20:27 NKJV). Follow in Paul's footsteps.

Preachers who are overly concerned about offending people and losing congregants, ironically end up losing some people anyway. Who? Mature believers. Why? Because, as believers begin to mature in their faith, many of them realize, "All I'm getting every week at this church is milk!" And they leave. Many of them settle down at churches that are committed to teaching in a more in-depth expository fashion.

D. Teaching verse-by-verse will help disarm your critics.

When you work your way through a portion of Scripture that deals with a controversial topic (Hell, homosexuality, giving, etc.), your listeners won't be tempted to think you have a "hidden agenda," i.e., that you are just trying to talk about one of your favorite subjects. They will realize, "This is just where we happen to be in our verse-by-verse examination of the Bible."

So, for these reasons, I encourage you to seriously consider teaching verse-by-verse.

12. Don't assume your listeners know the Bible better than they do.

"I fed you with milk, not solid food, for you were not ready for it. And even now you are not yet ready." (1 Cor. 3:2 esv)

It can be easy for pastors and teachers who are always reading and studying to forget how prevalent Biblical illiteracy is. What surveys show about Biblical illiteracy, even among Evangelicals, at least in America, is startling. An article in a 2010 edition of *Christianity Today* pointed out that:

> Most Americans—including Scripture-loving Evangelicals—cannot name the disciples, the Ten Commandments, or the first book of the Bible... *Time* magazine observed in a 2007 cover story that only half of U.S. adults could name one of the four Gospels.[25]

---

[25] Collin Hansen, "Why Johnny Can't Read the Bible," *Christianity Today*, May 24, 2010, http://www.christianitytoday.com/ct/2010/may/25.38.html.

Of course, the people we teach may fare better if *Time* magazine ever calls and asks them to take part in a survey. At least we'd like to hope so! But still, it's probably safe to say that very few of the people we teach:

- Have been to seminary or Bible college
- Study the Bible in an in-depth manner
- Own a Bible commentary, Bible dictionary or Bible encyclopedia

I think it's good to remember this as you're preparing sermons. If you assume people know the Bible better than they do, you can develop a tendency to skip over explaining things that seem elementary ("They know this already!").

Now, this isn't to say you should speak to your congregation like they're a newly discovered tribe on a remote island who has never had any exposure to the Bible—"This is a Biiiiible. B. I. B. L. E." No. I just encourage you to:

- Be prayerful about what you skip over
- Be thoughtful before you decide not to address something that seems basic to you
- Be careful about those things you are thinking about leaving out

Those truths may be the very truths that some of the people need to have explained or need to be reminded of. And going over what seems elementary to you will benefit the mature believers by way of reminder (2 Pet. 1:12–15).

For the sake of the mature believers who already have a good grasp on the elementary truths of the Christian faith, try to package the truth in fresh phrasing. Avoid using old, overused illustrations. Quote a verse or two that you don't usually quote (e.g., instead of Romans 3:23, try Isaiah 53:6). Avoid using old, worn out clichés like:

- "Grace is God's riches at Christ's expense"
- "He paid a debt He did not owe because we owed a debt we could not pay"

These are so overused they fail to deliver any punch with people who've heard them a hundred times.

13. As you study and prepare, ask the six big questions.

"Examining the Scriptures daily to see." (Acts 17:11)

In the days of Nehemiah, the Levites "read distinctly from the book, in the Law of God; and they gave the sense, and helped them to *understand* the reading" (Nehemiah 8:8 NKJV). That is one of the supreme goals for those who teach God's Word to others—helping people "*understand* the reading." How might one improve in his ability to help others understand the Bible?

As you read the Bible and begin to study and seek to know what a passage means, I encourage you to view yourself sort of like a newspaper reporter or private investigator. There are six big questions to be asking.

A. Who?

Who wrote the letter? Who was it written to? Who was involved in the events recorded?

B. What?

What happened? What ideas are expressed? What were the results?

C. Where?

Where did the recorded events take place? What is the geographical setting? The Bible can come alive in the minds of those you teach if you include a little background information on the city or geographical setting where something took place.

D. When?

When did the event take place? What is the historical background? Was it in Babylon during the exile? Was it during Paul's second missionary journey?

E. Why?

Why did it happen? Why did Elijah retreat into the wilderness after such a spectacular victory at Mount Carmel? Why did God allow the Babylonians to sack the city of Jerusalem? Is the purpose or reason it happened explained?

F. How?

How were things accomplished? How well? How quickly? By what method?

Those are the kinds of questions on the minds of our listeners. Hunting down answers to those questions and integrating them into your teachings will help your listeners leave with a much better understanding of the Bible.

14. Consider walking through these suggested steps when preparing a sermon.

There are a variety of ways to approach preparing a sermon. Here is a suggested guideline and the way I typically approach the task.

A. Choose the text.

Choosing a text is easy if you're teaching chapter-by-chapter, verse-by-verse. If your opportunity to teach is a special occasion (perhaps you've been invited to fill in for another teacher somewhere) and you are free to choose a topic or text:

- Pray for wisdom on what to teach (James 1:5)
- Consider the people you are going to address
- Consider the occasion
- Consider the time you will be allotted (10 minutes? 45 minutes?)
- Consider the need or dominant concerns of the people
- Consider what Scriptures have blessed you recently (sharing something you are excited about is beneficial for obvious reasons)

B. Prayerfully meditate on the text.

- Pray and ask God to help you think clearly about what the text says; pray that the eyes of your heart may be

opened to see wonderful things in the Word (Eph. 1:18; 2 Tim. 2:7)
- Read through the passage multiple times (eight to ten times is a good guideline)
- Turn it over and over again in your mind; let it soak in
- Scribble down your thoughts and initial insights on a piece of paper

C. Study the passage.

Look up cross-references. Compare Scripture with Scripture. Examine the context. Do as much research as you need to in commentaries, Bible dictionaries, background notes in Study Bibles, etc., to answer the *who, what, where, when, why* and *how* questions. Get a firm grasp on *what* the text says and what the text *means*.

D. Begin typing out your sermon.

I like to cut and paste the entire passage of Scripture (from Bible study software) that I will be covering into a blank document. I change the words of the Bible to a *blue* font to differentiate them from my comments. Then I begin plugging in my comments, notes, and the things I want to say in between the verses in *black* font. Using different color fonts for Scripture and my comments helps me keep better track of where I'm at as I prepare and as I teach.

Regarding fonts for your teaching notes, I like to use fonts with serifs, i.e., Minion or Times New Roman. Years ago I used the Arial font until I learned that fonts with serifs are considered easier to read. When I switched I noticed the difference. So, you may keep that in mind. Also, I encourage you to use a font size of thirteen or larger so you can easily see your notes when you are standing at the pulpit.

E. Prepare your conclusion and introduction.

I will have more to say about conclusions and introductions later on. I will give you one quick word of advice here. Prepare your conclusion and introduction *after* the body of the sermon is finished.

F. Print out a preliminary copy of your notes and go over them with a pencil.

Find some quiet time to prayerfully go over your notes with a pencil in hand. It is amazing how many things you will spot that you will want to change once you see your notes on paper. So, cross things off; write new notes in the margin. Be on the look out for things that are not worded clearly. Cross off things that are not necessary.

G. Go back to your computer and make the final changes to your notes.

H. Print out your finished notes. Highlight key words.

Once I have my finished notes in hand, I like to take a neon yellow highlighter and highlight key words or phrases in each paragraph and even draw small icons or symbols in the margins of my notes that will allow me to, with a glance, look down and recall a particular point as easily as possible. I dread being tied to my notes. The freer you are from your notes, the better!

I. Pray and commit the teaching to the Lord.

15. Make sure the verses you look at (or cite) actually support the point you are making when they are properly interpreted in their own context.

*"You are mistaken, not understanding
the Scriptures." (Matt. 22:29)*

When you are preparing a sermon and looking for verses that will support or add weight to a point you are making, it can be easy to inadvertently use a verse that does not actually support your point. The reason this can happen is because you are usually not spending as much time studying the context of those other peripheral passages.

Here's an example. You're teaching through Matthew 24. You come to the verse where Jesus said, "Heaven and earth will pass away, but My words will not pass away" (Matt. 24:35).

You notice that Jesus speaks here of the indestructibility of His words and you decide that you would like to show that this is something the Scriptures talk about elsewhere. So, you look up the word "preserve" in a concordance to see if there might be anywhere else in the Bible where God assures us that He will preserve His Word. There in your search results you see Psalm 12:7. It says:

You shall keep them, O Lord, You shall preserve them
from this generation forever (Psalm 12:7 NKJV).

"Oh, that looks interesting," you say. So, you quickly back up a verse to make sure the verse is speaking about the Word and verse six says:

> The words of the Lord are pure words, like silver tried in a furnace of earth, purified seven times (Psalm 12:6 NKJV).

"Perfect!" you say. So, you cut and paste verse seven right into your notes. Then you teach it. Unfortunately, you've just inadvertently mishandled the Bible. You've erred at rightly dividing God's Word (2 Tim. 2:15).

You stated something that is *true*—God will preserve His Word (Isa. 40:8)—but you used a verse that when correctly interpreted in its context does not support your point. I won't take the time to break down Psalm 12, but if you take a longer look at it on your own, you'll see that Psalm 12:7 is actually speaking about *people*, not the Scriptures.

You might say, "At least my point was true—although the verse did not support it." Yes, but there are some real dangers in making this kind of mistake.

A. Sloppy exposition can hurt your credibility

Some of your listeners who *have* studied Psalm 12 (or whatever other passage you cite) in its context will realize the error you're making and you will instantly lose some credibility with them. They will see your mishandling of God's Word—even though it was an honest mistake without any harm intended—and your credibility will suffer. This will make it harder for them to trust you in the future, even when you get it right.

B. Sloppy exposition can hurt a listener's confidence in the truth of Scripture

The next time your listener is reading through Psalm 12 on his own, he may discover the *real* meaning of the text and then lose confidence in the original truth you shared with him (God is going to preserve His Word).

This loss of confidence and resulting confusion is the fall-out of a teacher's sloppy handling of God's Word. If you want to avoid throwing out these kinds of "hermeneutical grenades"—interpretations that explode long after you've thrown them—I encourage you to make sure the verses you look at, cite, or quote actually support the point you are making when they are properly interpreted in their own context.

This is another reminder of why it is so important to know the Word. If you had previously studied Psalm 12 you would not have made the mistake.

16. Point people to Jesus.

"Fixing our eyes on Jesus."
(Heb. 12:2)

At the close of a service, a preacher was stopped by a gentleman who, after conceding that the sermon possessed certain commendable features, added, "But it had one noticeable defect!" The startled minister, on inquiring what this defect was, received the following reply: "I am a Jew. I have only recently been born again. Up to that time I attended the synagogue. But there was really nothing in your sermon that I could not have heard in the synagogue, nothing that a Jewish rabbi might not have preached." "That," said the preacher in later years, "was the greatest lesson in homiletics I was ever taught."[26]

It seems to me, based on feedback I am getting from God's people in different areas of North America, that there is a drought of Christ-centered preaching today—preaching that magnifies Jesus and extols His attributes, preaching that holds Him up and says to believers and nonbelievers alike, "Run to Jesus. He is your God! He is your help! He is your hope! He is your salvation! Turn to Him all the ends of the Earth and be saved!"

I'm afraid Mary might say the same thing in some churches today that she said standing outside the tomb on the morning of the resurrection, "They have taken away my Lord, and I do not know where they have laid Him" (John 20:13). Charles Spurgeon said:

> I have heard of ministers who can preach a sermon without mentioning the name of Jesus from beginning to end. If you ever hear such a sermon as that, mind that you never hear another from that man.[27]

Spurgeon said those words because the Bible is ultimately about our Lord and Savior, Jesus Christ. He Himself affirmed this to be the case in Luke 24. Luke writes:

> And beginning with Moses and with all the prophets, He [Jesus] explained to them the things concerning [Who?] *Himself* [Where?] in all the Scriptures...Now He said to them, "These are My words which I spoke to you while I

[26] *Illustrations of Bible Truths*, compiled by Ruth Peters, QuickVerse.

[27] Charles Spurgeon, "Great Forgiveness for Great Sin," a sermon delivered on December 31, 1876.

was still with you, that all things which are written about *Me* in the Law of Moses and the Prophets and the Psalms must be fulfilled" (Luke 24:27, 44).

On numerous occasions, the New Testament affirms that Jesus is *the* theme of Old Testament Scripture.[28]

Dr. Norman Geisler gives this concise summary of how all eight sections of the Bible point to Jesus.

- The Law. . . . . The **Foundation** is laid for Christ
- The Historical Books. . . . . **Preparation** for Christ
- The Poetical Books. . . . . . . **Aspiration** for Christ is expressed
- The Prophetical Books. . . . The **Expectation** of Christ
- The Gospels. . . . . The **Manifestation** of Christ
- The Book of Acts. . . . . The **Propagation** of Christ
- The Epistles. . . . . The **Interpretation** and **Application** of Christ
- The Book of Revelation. . . The **Consummation** of all things in Christ[29]

Truly, the Scriptures are Christocentric (Christ-centered). Jesus said, "You search the Scriptures, for in them you think you have eternal life; *and these are they which testify of Me. But you are not willing to come to Me that you may have life*" (John 5:39–40 NKJV).

In light of what Jesus says here and in the passage I quoted above in Luke 24, whenever you are preparing for a teaching, I encourage you to ask, *"How might this passage point to Jesus?"* The answer to that question is something you should prayerfully consider including in your teaching.

---

[28] Other references include: Matthew 5:17; John 1:45, 5:39, 46; Hebrews 10:7; Acts 2:30–31, 3:18, 10:43, 17:2–3; 1 Cor. 10:4, 15:3–4; 1 Peter 1:10–11.
[29] Norman L. Geisler, *A Popular Survey of the Old Testament*, 21–24.

Having said that, don't mistakenly think that every verse in the Bible speaks directly or explicitly of Jesus. That is not what Jesus meant in Luke 24:27 or John 5:39. Every text of Scripture is part of the *one story*, which has its ultimate focus in Him, but not every verse.

17. Know there are typically at least five types of people in the average gathering.

"All Scripture is inspired by God and profitable for teaching, for reproof, for correction, for training in righteousness." (2 Tim. 3:16)

In the average gathering of God's people on a Sunday morning, there at least five different types of people, spiritually speaking, that you'll want to have in mind when you are preparing to teach.

A. Mature spiritual believers (1 Cor. 3:1; Heb. 5:14)
B. Struggling or hurting believers
C. Immature ("Babes in Christ" 1 Cor. 3:1)
D. Carnal believers ("still fleshly" 1 Cor. 3:3)
E. Nonbelievers

When preaching, there is always the danger of narrowing your comments and exhortation to only one or two groups. That should not be the case. Seek as much as possible to speak to all five groups. Here are some of their basic needs:

A. Mature spiritual believers (1 Cor. 3:1; Heb. 5:14)

They can handle and *need* insights into the Word that are meatier ("solid food" Heb. 5:12, 14) than what younger believers need. They need more than the "elementary principles" (Heb. 5:12) or the basics of Christianity. They want to learn things they have not seen on their own. They will grow weak with "milk" (1 Cor. 3:2) week after week. And that is what is happening in some churches today. Pastors are aiming their messages at the unchurched and new believers. And many of the mature believers are leaving malnourished.

B. Struggling or hurting believers (young and old in the faith)

The world has been hard on people. The effects of sin have taken a toll on them. Their hearts are broken over relationships that have ended. They are worried about finding work, finances, their wayward kids, etc. Seek to encourage them. They need "exhortation and consolation" (1 Cor. 14:3). It's rightly been said, "Preach to the hurting and you will always have a congregation."

C. Immature ("Babes in Christ" 1 Cor. 3:1)

Immature believers need to grow in their understanding of the basic, elementary doctrines of the Christian faith. So, make sure to explain some of those when appropriate. Some of the old saints might grumble in their hearts ("We already know this") but if you teach the basics in an interesting way (e.g., with fresh illustrations or quotes you haven't used before) they shouldn't mind hearing them again.

D. Carnal believers ("Still fleshly" 1 Cor. 3:3)

The carnal need to be challenged to abandon areas of compromise and sin and to live their lives wholeheartedly for the Lord.

E. Nonbelievers:

Nonbelievers need to be given the gospel (Rom. 1:15–16). They need to be told to repent (Acts 17:30) and to trust in Jesus (Roman 10:9–10). They need to be warned about a coming judgment (Acts 24:25) and the eternal consequences of refusing God's offer of salvation (Rom. 2:5–6).

If you are teaching a small group and are confident that everybody is saved, then giving a detailed explanation of the gospel every week is not necessary. If there is someone new there though and you are unsure of his or her spiritual condition, make sure to share the gospel. He may never have another chance to hear it.

18. When you are preparing your sermon, be sure to consult with other translations of the Bible.

"Different translations can help you see a text with fresh eyes."[30] *–H. B. Charles*

There were some times in my earlier years of teaching, that I would jot down some thoughts, even develop a point in my sermon notes, only to realize *after* I read the same passage in a

---

[30] H. B. Charles, Jr., "My Journey to the English Standard Version," http://www.hbcharlesjr.com/2012/08/07/my-journey-to-the-english-standard-version.

different translation that I had a slight misunderstanding of the text.

This is a common mistake that young and even experienced teachers can make. The error can be avoided by reading the passage early on in a handful of different translations. Where the New King James Version may be kind of unclear, the English Standard Version or the New American Standard may be clearer and vice-versa.

I recommend you read the passage you are going to teach in at least five of these different translations:

- The New King James Version (NKJV)
- The English Standard Version (ESV)
- The New American Standard Version (NASB)
- The Amplified Bible (AMP)
- The King James Version (KJV)
- The New International Version (NIV)
- The New Living Translation (NLT)

Not only will doing this help you avoid a faulty interpretation, it will help you develop a proper interpretation of the passage. Although the NIV and NLT are not literal "word-for-word" translations, they can still be helpful. I stay away from *The Message* translation. It reads like a sermon (text plus interpretation and application). Unlike a sermon, however, the reader does not know where the text ends and the sermon begins.[31]

An easy way to compare multiple Bible translations side by side is to type in a verse reference at Biblos.com. There is also excellent Bible study software by Logos and Biblesoft.[32] I'll talk

---

[31] See John R. Kohlenberger III, "The Message Bible: A Book Review of *The Message* by Eugene Peterson," http://www.equip.org/articles/the-message-bible.

[32] Available at Logos.com and BibleSoft.com.

more about software later.

19. Deal with the difficulties in the passage you are teaching.

"Some things in them [Paul's writings]...are hard to understand, which the ignorant and unstable twist to their own destruction." (2 Pet. 3:16)

Let's imagine you are starting off a teaching in First Peter. So, for your first teaching, you give of an introduction to the epistle. You talk about who wrote the letter, who it was written to, when it was written, etc. That's great. Then you begin your verse-by-verse journey through the first chapter:

> Peter, an apostle of Jesus Christ, to the pilgrims of the Dispersion in Pontus, Galatia, Cappadocia, Asia, and Bithynia, elect according to the foreknowledge of God the Father, in sanctification of the Spirit, for obedience and sprinkling of the blood of Jesus Christ: Grace to you and peace be multiplied (1 Peter 1:1–2 NKJV).

Now, there are some confusing things Peter wrote there. If you quickly pass over them and summarize these two verses with some brief comment like, "Well, here we see that God has elected us and desires to sanctify us, that we might be obedient" and then you jump into verse three, you are going to frustrate your listeners. Many of your listeners are going to be asking...

- What is "the Dispersion"?
- What does it mean to be "elect"?

66

- What does Peter mean when he says that we were elect "according to the *foreknowledge* of God"?
- What is Peter talking about when he says the "sprinkling of the blood of Jesus"?

To read through a passage like this and just restate the obvious or quickly restate the verse in different words is to miss the point of teaching. *Anybody can do that!* There is nothing more frustrating for many listeners than for a teacher to constantly avoid the difficult questions that passages of Scripture bring up in their minds. Any teacher can carry on about the obvious. A good teacher will deal with the difficulties in the passage and seek to make them clear.

Now this doesn't mean you need to deal with *every* difficulty in a passage.

- You may realize your listeners are already familiar with the topic
- You may have just taught on the difficult topic
- You may be planning on teaching on the topic in a future study where it will be more appropriate to discuss (In that case, it might be good to let people know that)

It's not hard to spot the difficulties in a passage. The first or second time you read through a passage you're planning on teaching, ask yourself prior to looking at any commentaries:

- What don't I understand in the passage?

And write those thoughts down. Then read through it again and ask yourself:

- What wouldn't a new believer understand in this passage?

Doing that will help you put together a list of questions you should prayerfully consider answering in your teaching.

20. Evaluate your conclusions in reliable sources.

"It seems odd, that certain men who talk so much of what the Holy Spirit reveals to themselves, should think so little of what He has revealed to others."[33] *–Charles Spurgeon*

It is rare that I will ever preach a sermon or take a study to the pulpit without having first checked my conclusions (interpretations) with scholars and teachers who know the Bible better than I do.

I learned early on how important this is. It is amazing how you can think you have a clear understanding of what a passage is about, when actually that is not the case.

We are called to "rightly divide" God's Word (2 Tim. 2:15). So, before you accidentally share something with God's people that is not accurate, I encourage you to *check with the experts.*

This is why it is important to have a good library. I'll talk more about owning good books later on.

---

[33] Charles Spurgeon, *Commenting and Commentaries*, 1.

21. Don't just tell your listeners *what* a passage means; show them *why* it means that.

"He reasoned with them from the Scriptures,
explaining and proving that it was necessary for
the Christ to suffer and to rise from the dead."
(Acts 17:2–3 ESV)

It's important to tell people *how* you have arrived at a particular interpretation—*why* you believe a passage means what you say it means. Give them reasons. Show them how your conclusions harmonize with what the Bible teaches elsewhere.

Now, obviously this is not something you need to do with every passage. With a verse like, "Love one another" (1 Jn. 4:11), you don't need to prove that this really means we should love one another. The meaning is quite plain. Your time would be better spent sharing some practical ways we can love one another, some Biblical examples of this virtue being lived out, etc.

However, when you are teaching on passages that are not so clear (cf. 2 Pet. 3:16), or where there are a range of different interpretations, it is wise to lay out the reasons you hold to a particular interpretation. Doing this will not only help your listeners have a better grasp on what the Bible teaches, it will help them learn how to study the Bible for themselves.

22. Consider these seven steps as a possible framework for the delivery of your sermon.

In my opinion, most good sermons pass through seven phases— whether the teacher or listener realizes it or not. Becoming familiar with these seven phases may help those of you who are new to teaching. Phases A, B, and C can be rearranged into the order of your choosing.

A. **Opening prayer**

B. **Introduction**

C. **The reading of the passage**

D. **The breaking down and explaining of the passage, often accompanied by an illustration or two**

E. **Application** (Helping listeners to understand how the passage might apply to their lives)

   Phases C, D, and E may repeat as you make your way through additional Scripture.

F. **Concluding exhortation**[34]

G. **Closing prayer**

---

[34] I will have more to say about conclusions later on.

23. Preach a big God.

"For the LORD is a great God and a great
King above all gods." (Ps. 95:3)

I love to look up at the stars on a dark night and ponder the enormity of the universe. Surely, "The heavens declare the glory of God" (Ps. 19:1). Consider a few staggering facts. If we were to hollow out the inside of the Sun, we could place more than one million Earths inside. The Sun is huge, 866 *thousand* miles wide. But astronomers tell us the star Betelgeuse[35] is much bigger—215 *million* miles wide! But they say that VY Canis Majoris is even larger—more than a *billion* miles across. If we were to replace our Sun with this star, its surface would extend to the orbit of Saturn.[36] That means that Earth could continue on its orbit inside this star. Now, as enormous as VY Canis Majoris is, keep in mind this is just a single star in our Milky Way Galaxy.

Today, with the help of the Hubble Space Telescope, scientists estimate that the Milky Way contains approximately two hundred billion stars! And scientists estimate that there are more than 100 billion other galaxies in the universe containing anywhere from a billion to more than a *trillion* stars each![37]

Friends, I think it's safe to say that the universe is larger than any of us have ever realized and that God is far more powerful than we've ever imagined. I don't know about you, but when I consider the heavens and realize afresh who it is I'm telling people about, I want to preach a "big" God.

---

[35] Pronounced "beetle juice."

[36] http://hubblesite.org/newscenter/archive/releases/2007/03/full/.

[37] http://www.nasa.gov/worldbook/galaxy_worldbook.html.

One of the reasons why some Christians struggle with fear or grow lukewarm in their desire to worship God is because they are harboring thoughts about God that fall far short of who He really is. In other words, their God is too small.

God forbid we aid their small god mentality with our preaching. Warren and David Wiersbe give an appropriate word of advice regarding this matter, "Don't strive to prepare and preach "great sermons" but to magnify a great Savior."[38] Their exhortation to preach a "great Savior" reminds me of the Psalmist's words: "Let those who love Thy salvation say continually, "The LORD be magnified (Psalm 40:16b)!" That should be one of our goals when we preach, magnifying the Lord, talking glowingly about His attributes and His great deeds, helping people to understand how great our God really is.

We should dread the thought that people will walk away from our teachings thinking, "That was a great sermon." It would be far better if they left thinking, "What a great God we have!" Make that a goal in your teaching. Magnify the Lord.

Richard Mayhue, of The Master's Seminary in California, was given a note some time ago. He opened the note and it said, "Brother, don't ever try to be a big preacher. Instead preach a big Savior."[39] What great advice! We have a big Savior. Let's tell people about Him.

---

[38] Warren Wiersbe and David Wiersbe, *The Elements of Preaching*, 44.

[39] Richard L. Mayhue, "Introductions, Illustrations, and Conclusions," in *Rediscovering Expository Preaching*, 246.

24. Try to emphasize what *God* has done for the people not what *people* have done for God.

"To the praise and glory of His
grace, which He freely bestowed on us
in the Beloved." (Eph. 1:6)

One of our goals as shepherds and teachers of God's people is to help them make *God* the focus of their lives. We want them to run the race looking unto Jesus, the author and perfecter of their faith (Heb. 12:2). I trust you agree with me on that. But there is a possibility in our preaching that even knowing the above to be true, we put the focus on a man (a Scriptural character) or the great qualities and characteristics of a particular *person* instead of upon the God who made that person great.

There is nothing wrong with doing character studies that look at the lives of particular individuals in the Bible. There is much we can learn from what is written about them. But we need to be careful as we examine their lives, their heroics and accomplishments (e.g., Joseph's rise to power in Egypt, Gideon's routing of the Midianites) to shine the spotlight on the Lord and what *He* did in the person's life and situation. He alone, really, is the hero of every story in the Bible.

As great of a man as we believe the apostle Paul was, in reality apart from God's grace:

- He was the chief of sinners (1 Tim. 1:15)
- He was a wretched man (Rom. 7:24)
- There was nothing good that dwelt in his flesh (Rom. 7:18)

Knowing that to be the case, we don't want people to leave our teachings enamored with Paul—or any other man. We want them to walk away from our teachings glorifying God who did great things in and through these men. God was and is the only praise-worthy one (Matt. 19:17).

25. Be accurate with statistics.

"Having investigated everything carefully."
(Luke 1:3)

I've written elsewhere about the importance of being accurate when interpreting the Bible,[40] but it is also important to be accurate when you include statistics in your study. Statistics can be good.

- They let us know how a certain segment of society thinks
- They let us understand how the population behaves and feels about certain issues
- They allow us to follow trends

But, if you are going to maintain your credibility, you need to be careful to not throw around statistics that are outdated, not accurate, hearsay, etc. Here are two quick examples:

Earthquakes Are On the Rise?

You have probably heard that earthquakes are on the rise worldwide and that this is a fulfillment of Matthew 24:7. I hear Christians saying this everywhere I go after a major

---

[40] See my article "Rules and Guidelines by Which to Properly Interpret the Bible" in our "Hermeneutics" section at AlwaysBeReady.com.

earthquake. Well, the experts say otherwise and they have lots of data to back it up. The U. S. Geological Survey (earthquake.usgs.gov) says:

> Although it may seem that we are having more earthquakes, earthquakes of magnitude 7.0 or greater have remained fairly constant...Because of the improvements in communications and the increased interest in the environment and natural disasters, the public now learns about more earthquakes. According to long-term records (since about 1900), we expect about 17 major earthquakes (7.0 - 7.9) and one great earthquake (8.0 or above) in any given year.[41]

In an interview in the *Washington Post*, Dr. Michael Blanpied, with the USGS, explained:

> There are really three main reasons why we're seeing more news about deadly earthquakes. First is that the quality of reporting is much higher. Second is that we're able to record them better due to global digital seismic networks that report data in real time. Third is that more and more people live in quake-prone areas, so earthquakes are more likely to strike vulnerable populations than was the case decades ago.[42]

The Institute for Creation Research (ICR), a Christian scientific research group, has also documented that earthquakes are

---

[41] U. S. Geological Survey, "Are Earthquakes Really on the Increase?" July 18, 2012, http://earthquake.usgs.gov/learn/topics/increase_in_earthquakes.php.

[42] Dr. Michael Blanpied, "Seismic Science: Is number of earthquakes on the rise?" March 9, 2010, http://www.washingtonpost.com/wp-dyn/content/discussion/2010/03/08/DI2010030802570.html.

not on the rise. Dr. Steven Austin, the chairman of the geology department at ICR, addresses this issue on their website.[43]

Christians Divorce as Much as Non-Christians?

Another statistic that is commonly cited in pulpits is that the divorce rate amongst Christians is as high as among non-Christians: 50 percent! Before you say something like that, it would be good to do some research and find out if any actual studies have produced reliable data to back that up. And when you do, you discover that this often stated "fact" is not true.

The divorce rate amongst Christians in America *is* alarming but it is nowhere near 50%.[44] Statistics say that the number is more like 26%. The Barna Group research service says:

> The groups with the most prolific experience of marriage ending in divorce are downscale adults (39%), Baby Boomers (38%), those aligned with a non-Christian faith (38%), African-Americans (36%), and people who consider themselves to be liberal on social and political matters (37%). Among the population segments with the lowest likelihood of having been divorced subsequent to marriage are Catholics (28%), **evangelicals (26%)**, upscale adults (22%), Asians (20%) and those who deem themselves to be conservative on social and political matters (28%).[45]

---

[43] See: http://www.icr.org/article/earthquakes-these-last-days. And http://www.icr.org/article/twentieth-century-earthquakes-confronting-urban-le/.

[44] I did not look into divorce statistics for other countries, seeing that I do not know what teachers outside of the USA are saying about the matter.

[45] Barna Group, "New Marriage and Divorce Statistics Released" http://barna.org/barna-update/article/15-familykids/42-new-marriage-and-divorce-statistics-released. March 31, 2008.

Bradford Wilcox, a leading sociologist at the University of Virginia and Director of the National Marriage Project found in 2007, that active, conservative members of Protestant churches are 35 percent less likely to divorce than Americans who are religiously unaffiliated.[46] The urban legend-busting website TruthorFiction.com has come up with similar statistics as well and called the 50% statistic "a tragically discouraging urban legend."[47]

My fellow preachers, before you include statistics in your study, ask a few questions:

- Who says?
- Who counted?
- Who was counted?[48]
- When?
- Where?

And tell your listeners some of those facts so that they can make up their own mind. For example, rather than just coming out and saying: "38% of Americans believe (fill in the blank). Say something like, "According to the Gallup polling organization, who surveyed 30,000 adults from all around the United States in 1998, 38% of Americans believe such and such."

---

[46] John Stonestreet, "Busting the Myth: Christians and Divorce" October 5, 2012, http://www.breakpoint.org/bpcommentaries/entry/13/20460?tmpl =component&print=1.

[47] See: http://www.truthorfiction.com/rumors/d/divorce.htm.

[48] Was the survey done among 100 inmates in a prison somewhere? Was the survey done in just one city? These factors can skew the numbers.

26. Be accurate with stories.

"Speaking the truth in love." (Eph. 4:15)

In addition to being careful with statistics (see previous point), be careful to avoid using "urban legends" in your messages. Urban legends are those fascinating stories that often circulate via email *that are not true*. They sound true and they are tempting to use. And many a teacher has unwittingly used one in a sermon. Let me share with you some of the ones I have heard teachers share.

• Evangelist on Doomed Alaska Airline

A woman supposedly preached to the people on board the Alaska Airlines plane that went down on January 31, 2000, off the coast of California, for the final 9 minutes of their lives, finally leading them in a prayer. It was apparently captured on a recording. *Not true.*

• The *Harry Potter* Author is a Satanist

A report came out that author, J. K. Rowling, is a Satanist, set on deceiving children and drawing Christian kids away from the Lord and into sacrificing animals. Well, the story came from an article in *The Onion*, a newspaper that purposely publishes satire—outrageous and untrue stories for laughs.[49]

• The Beast Computer

---

[49] "Harry Potter Books Spark Rise In Satanism Among Children" July 26, 2000. http://www.theonion.com/articles/harry-potter-books-spark-rise-in-satanism-among-ch,2413/.

This was supposedly a gigantic three-story computer in Brussels, Belgium, that had the capability to track every sale in the world. *Not true.*

- **Charles Darwin**

Charles Darwin repented and embraced Christianity on his deathbed. *Not true.*

- **NASA's Discovery of a Missing Day**

NASA found a "missing day" on the calendar, explained only by the Bible. *Not true.* NASA has issued a statement flatly denying that any such discovery ever took place.[50]

- **Swallowed by a Whale**

A nineteenth century whaler was swallowed by a whale and recovered alive, thus proving the possibility of the account of Jonah. *Not true.*

- **Al Gore's Favorite Verse**

Former Vice President, Al Gore, said that his favorite Bible verse was John 16:3 during a campaign speech. In this verse, Jesus says, "They will do such things because they have not known the Father or me." *Not true.*

- **Rapture Proof Aircraft**

---

[50] NASA, "Ask an Astrophysicist" March 25, 1997, http://imagine.gsfc.nasa.gov/docs/ask_astro/answers/970325g.html.

Airline companies schedule Christian pilots with a non-Christian crew in case the Christian disappears in the Rapture. *Not true.*

- **Evangelist George W. Bush**

Former President George W. Bush took time at a banquet to help a teen become a Christian. *Not true.*

These stories sound great, but all of them were made up. If you, even unknowingly, include these kinds of inaccurate stories in your teachings your credibility will plummet amongst the well-read and well-informed (not to mention people listening to you with their iPads and web browsers open, ready to fact-check you). You do not want to do anything that will undermine your credibility as a reliable source of truth. Non-believers, who often are looking for reasons to *not* believe you, will have good reason should they know the truth behind these kinds of stories.

So, be careful. If you're not confident something is trustworthy, don't share it. Be like Luke who "investigated everything carefully...so that you might know the *exact truth* about the things you have been taught" (Luke 1:3–4). Check with reliable, original sources and verify the facts. TruthorFiction.com and Snopes.com are helpful websites. Often times, they will tell you whether a story is true or just a fabrication and how they came to their conclusion.

27. Avoid alliterating your points.

*"How will people ponder the beauty of our Lord
if they are thinking about the cleverness of the
preacher?" –the author*

Using the same letter over and over in your main points is called *alliteration*. A pastor's outline or list of his main points might look like this:

1. Jesus Was Praying to God (Lk. 5:16)
2. Jesus Was Preaching of God (5:17a)
3. Jesus Was Powered by God (5:17b)
4. Jesus Was Present as God (5:17c)
5. Jesus Was Passionate Like God (5:18–26)
6. Justin the Preacher Passed Out Unlike God...from exhaustion trying to think up so many "P" words.

Alliteration has become a very popular practice in the pulpit, but in most cases I believe it should be avoided. I used to be a fervent alliterator (My computer is telling me that *alliterator* is not a word and is offering *obliterator* as an alternative. Ha!). Well, let me give you seven reasons why I obliterated my previous practice of alliterating my studies:

A. Jesus didn't teach this way, nor did the prophets or the disciples.

That alone is reason enough for me. Add to this the fact that none of us ever talk this way in every day life and the issue is settled for me.

B. Alliteration draws attention to the cleverness of the preacher.

As a teacher shares his alliterated points, people often sit there and think, *"Wow. That is cool. All those words start with the same letter. That's amazing. I wonder how he thinks of those!"*

Is that what we want people thinking while we teach—how clever we are? Our supreme goal in teaching is to *glorify God*, not to appear clever. How will people ponder the beauty of our Lord if they are thinking about the cleverness of the preacher?

Someone came up to me once after I preached an alliterated sermon and said, "That was great how you got all of those words to start with S." That was the beginning of my change in belief regarding alliteration. As he was telling me this, I thought to myself, "He seems more impressed with *me* than with what the Bible had to say." That was a horrifying thought to me. John said, *"He* must increase, but I must *decrease"* (John 3:30).

C. The people you are teaching will think you are borrowing material.

On more than one occasion, after I taught studies that were alliterated, someone came to me and asked, *"Where did you get those points?"* or *"Did you come up with that outline all by yourself?"* Knowing I didn't have an advanced degree in communication, they assumed, "He must be borrowing his material from someone else." And if you alliterate your points, your listeners will probably suspiciously wonder the same thing, *"Does he really study or does he just get his messages from some sermon website?"*

Well, God forbid that people think we are just cut and paste sermon makers who do not love and interact with God's Word personally.

D. Alliteration isn't that helpful in aiding people's memories.

One of the number one reasons why some teachers try to alliterate their points is because they believe it aids their listener's memories. In other words, alliteration helps people remember the main points of the teaching. That's one of the reasons I used to alliterate. But it dawned on me, while I was wondering about the effectiveness of alliteration, that I could not remember any of the outlines I ever heard that were alliterated. Can you? I can hardly remember any of my *own* studies that I alliterated!

E. Alliteration can discourage potential teachers.

There will be men and women there amongst your listeners who are considering helping out in the children's ministry or starting a Bible study at work or in their homes. And when they hear your sermon brimming with all its cleverness, rhymes and alliterated points, some of them will think, "I could never have come up with that kind of an outline. I must not be called to do this." Your alliteration may discourage other laborers from joining in the work of teaching.

I love Pastor Chuck Smith of Calvary Chapel Costa Mesa, California. I love his teaching style. I have never heard him alliterate a sermon. He reads the Word. He gives explanation and exhortation and then moves on to the next verse, chapter after chapter, book after book. He keeps it simple. And his simplicity has inspired hundreds of men to pursue teaching others the Word. They listen to Pastor Chuck and they think, "With God's help I might be able to do this."

F. Alliteration tempts one to twist the text.

When you have four points you have managed to alliterate with the letter M, what happens when you come to the fifth point and no matter how hard you try, there is not an M word that works? Well, the temptation will be to de-emphasize (or emphasize) something that *is* (or isn't) there, in order to make the outline work. This is not the way to handle God's Word.

G. Alliteration takes up valuable time.

Thinking up points that start with the same letter takes time, time that would be better spent, in my opinion, studying the text and praying for the people who will hear the message. So, for these reasons, I encourage you to avoid alliteration.

28. Don't take your listeners on seemingly endless page flipping tours through the Bible.

> *"I have many more things to say to you, but you cannot bear them now."*
> *(John 16:12)*

When I teach, I like to build a case from the Bible that a particular point I'm making is truly what the Scriptures teach. I don't want people to believe something because *I* told them so. I want them to believe something because they've seen and been convinced that the Scriptures teach it.

To accomplish this, I will often have the congregation look at three or four verses that support the case I'm making. For example, if my point is "Jesus is mankind's only Savior," I might have the congregation read:

- Peter's words in Acts 4:12
  "There is salvation in no one else"

- John the Baptist's words in John 3:36
  "He who does not obey the Son will not see life"

- Jesus' words in John 14:6
  "No one comes to the Father but through Me"

Reading or quoting cross-references can:

- Add credibility to your interpretation
- Strengthen the point you are making
- Demonstrate the harmony that exists in the Scriptures
- Help sink a truth into your listener's minds
- Give people a longer time to consider what is being said

Now having said this, there's a pitfall to avoid when sharing cross-references and many an inexperienced teacher has fallen head first into the pit, including yours truly.

The trip into the pit usually goes down like this. The well-meaning preacher reads a passage of Scripture. Then, thinking he really needs to build a case for something, he has the people turn to another supporting verse. He reads it and off he is to the next verse, pausing just long enough to read it and maybe make a brief comment. So far, so good, but don't think he's done. No, no. He's just getting warmed up. And so he pushes on to the next verse, and the next, and the next, all the while believing that the cumulative weight of all those Scriptures and the swiftness at which the truth is going forth is really going to bless people. Well, it doesn't bless them. It frustrates them.

After the fourth or fifth verse, people stop turning in their Bibles. Their eyes begin to glaze over. They start scribbling absentmindedly on the back of the bulletin. They're checking emails on their phones. They're wondering what the football scores are. Why? The preacher is overloading them too quickly with too much information. And they understood and agreed with the case the preacher was seeking to build after the second or third verse. They didn't need all ten verses. Three or four would have been sufficient.

Now, of course, it's fine to take your listeners on a lengthy, carefully paced, guided tour through the Bible. But along the way you're making some comments; clarifying what the passages mean, providing illustrations when necessary, talking about how the truth might apply to believers in particular circumstances, etc. If you'll teach that way, people will joyfully give you their attention for a much longer period of time.

29. Remember that where the Scriptures are silent, speculation is not necessary.

"We are never preaching when we are hazarding speculations…Preaching is the proclamation of the Word."[51]
–G. Campbell Morgan

God has given mankind all we need to know to be saved and to live a godly life (2 Pet. 1:3). God surely could have given us all kinds of other details regarding an innumerable amount of other matters (Jn. 20:30). The Bible could be a collection of thousands of books, rather than the 66 we have. But it's not.

---

[51] G. Campbell Morgan, *Preaching*, 30.

God, in His wisdom, knows just what we need to know (Deut. 29:29).

In spite of the fact that there is plenty to know in the Bible and an abundance of material therein to preach on, we can all find it tempting to speculate about things God has chosen not to reveal. To speculate is to form a theory or conjecture about a subject without firm evidence. I once heard a teaching where the pastor speculated on where Heaven might be, saying it was likely in some northern area of space where astronomers say there are few stars. Well, the Bible does not say where Heaven is. It only indicates that it is up (e.g., 2 Ki. 2:11, Jn. 6:41). To go beyond that is to go beyond what the Bible says. Another teacher I heard tried to build a case for a particular angel slicing the curtain in the temple at the time of the crucifixion. It was all speculation. Others have talked about how old we will appear in Heaven, how long Jesus' hair was, etc.

Before you speculate or share your opinions on issues like these that the Bible is silent on, please keep in mind that doing so is unnecessary and can be detrimental to your listeners and others. Why?

Oftentimes, a teacher's *speculations* or theories end up becoming his listener's *beliefs!* And listener's beliefs are commonly the things they share with others. And on down the line it goes. Is this what we want—people believing and sharing speculation?—things that may not even be true?—ideas that have no firm evidence to support them? Do we want to be the architects of theories that grow into urban legends? God forbid! We want our listener's faith to be "established in *the truth*" (2 Pet. 1:12).

Those who stand before God's people to teach are to be preachers of "the Word" (2 Tim. 4:2), not speculators of the unknowable. We are to be proclaimers of "all that [Jesus] commanded" (Matt. 28:20), not heralds of the unknown.

30. Be careful with how often you refer to the Greek and Hebrew.

"His name in Hebrew is Abaddon, and in Greek he is called Apollyon." (Rev. 9:11)

I'm often asked if I know Hebrew or Greek. I like to tell people "I know a little Greek and a little Hebrew. The little Hebrew was our tour guide in Israel. The little Greek has a wonderful restaurant across town." But in all seriousness, I want to offer a quick word here on referring to the original languages in your teachings. I agree with Bryan Chapell that, "Excellent preaching makes people confident that biblical truth lies within their reach, not beyond their grasp."[52] You do not want to give your listeners the impression they need a seminary education or degrees in Hebrew and Greek to obtain a deep understanding of God's Word.

As I mention elsewhere in this book, our goal is not to impress our listeners. There's nothing wrong with occasionally referring to a Greek, Aramaic, or Hebrew word (Rev. 9:11), but I encourage moderation. Once or twice per teaching, if at all, is a good guideline. Referring to the original languages multiple times will likely create the impression that God's Word is a complicated labyrinth of dark passageways that only theologians and experts in foreign languages can successfully navigate. When you do that, you discourage Bible reading and study. And we certainly do not want that.

---

[52] Bryan Chapell, *Christ-Centered Preaching*, 106.

THE PREPARATION OF THE INTRODUCTION

31. Make your introductions interesting, short and clear.

"The main purpose of the introduction is to create interest and convince the listener that he can be helped by hearing your message."[53]
–Warren Wiersbe

As you walk up to the pulpit, there are dozens of things each person seated before you can decide to think about or do. They

---

[53] Warren Wiersbe and David Wiersbe, *The Elements of Preaching*, 75.

can listen to you or they can:

- Text their friends
- Work on a to-do list
- Doodle on the back of the bulletin
- Read the Bible on their own
- Pass notes
- Surf the web or play games on their phone
- Get up for a long trip to the restroom
- Visit the church's cafe
- Sleep

As they begin to ponder whether or not they are going to give you their undivided attention, many of them have an unspoken question on their mind, "Why should I listen to this message?" They will often determine what they are going to do within the first couple minutes of your message. If you bore them or fail to grab their attention, you risk losing them for much of the message. The best way to ensure people listen to what you have to say is to have a compelling introduction.

A good introduction can convince them that they can be helped by hearing what is about to be read (the Scriptures) and said (the teaching).[54] In his book, *Biblical Preaching*, Haddon Robinson says this about introductions:

You must turn voluntary attention into involuntary attention. When you start, the people listen because they *ought* to listen, but before long, you must motivate them to listen because they *can't help* but listen.[55]

---

[54] Adapted from Wiersbe, *The Elements of Preaching*, 75.

[55] Haddon Robinson, *Biblical Preaching*, 168.

There are many ways to begin a message. You can:

- Read Scripture
- Give some brief background on the text (the setting, the year, the author, etc.)
- Make a reference to a current event
- Share a personal story
- Ask the congregation a question or two (questions you plan on answering during the message)

Whatever you say, make sure the opening couple of minutes are interesting.

In a study I teach on evidence for the trustworthiness of the Bible, I don't just kick things off by sharing the first evidence. I start off with a series of questions: Why do you trust the Bible? What evidence do you have that it can be trusted? What about other books like the Qur'an and the Book of Mormon? What makes the Bible any different than those books? Hasn't the Bible been changed down through the centuries as it was translated and copied?

These are challenging questions to answer—questions that many people aren't prepared to answer. Starting off a teaching with questions like these helps create interest. People realize that they could use some help in this area. Knowing that one day they might face these kinds of questions, causes many to sit up, grab a pen for note taking, and lean in to hear more.

As you consider potential introductions to your teaching, ask yourself these questions:

A. Does it fit the occasion?

You don't want to start off with a joke to introduce a message about Hell or death.

B. Does it actually introduce the subject of my message?

C. Do I deliver in the message what I promise in the introduction?

D. Is it short?

Think of your introduction as an appetizer in relation to the main course.

E. Does it create the highest possible level of interest to capture the congregation's attention?

F. Is the introduction clear and striking? [56]

Your introduction should be crystal clear. Imagine picking up a book and wondering if it's going to be worth your time reading. What do you do? You look at the table of contents, read the first paragraph or, if you have the time, you read the introduction. If you're confused by what is said there, what are you going to do? Put the book down. The same is true with your introductions. If you are unclear or uninteresting, you are going to lose people.

---

[56] These questions are adapted from Richard Mayhue's chapter, "Introductions, Illustrations, and Conclusions," in *Rediscovering Expository Preaching*, 245–246.

32. Prepare your introduction at the end of your studying.

"The preface to a book is always the last thing written."[57] *–G. Campbell Morgan*

The best time, generally, to prepare an introduction for your sermon is *after* you've prepared the rest of the message. You don't want to work hard preparing a fantastic introduction early on in your preparation only to abandon it later in the week after you realize more clearly what you are actually going to be emphasizing in your teaching. Your study time is too valuable to be wasting time with introductions that end up on the cutting room floor.

So, I encourage you to do all of your studying and preparation. Then, having become familiar with the content of your message, you will know better *what* you're introducing.

Obviously, if you think you have a great idea for an introduction before you're done studying, jot it down. You might end up using it.

---

[57] G. Campbell Morgan, *Preaching*, 127.

THE PREPARATION OF THE ILLUSTRATIONS

33. Use illustrations wisely.

"When amateur communicators see lost looks on the faces of their listeners they say, 'Let me repeat myself.' Effective preachers respond to those lost looks with the words, 'Let me illustrate.'"[58] *–J. Kent Edwards*

Jesus is history's greatest teacher. So, when it comes to teaching, we do well to look to the Master and learn from Him. And it is interesting to note how often and how well Jesus used illustrations to aid His listener's understanding of an important point.

---

[58] J. Kent Edwards, *Deep Preaching*, 168.

It was not uncommon for Him to relate what He was saying to facts about sparrows, lilies, camels, seeds, white washed tombs, etc. And for good reason:

- Illustrations make a sermon interesting
- Illustrations make a point more memorable
- Illustrations make a point more convincing (some respond better to pictures than facts)
- Illustrations make a point more clear and understandable
- Illustrations can make a truth motivating
- Illustrations can help activate the hearing of the disinterested
- Illustrations involve all the human senses in the communication process[59]
- Illustrations transform the abstract into the concrete, the ancient into the modern, the unfamiliar into the familiar, the general into the particular, the vague into the precise, the unreal into the real, and the invisible into the visible[60]

These are all good reasons to use illustrations in your teachings. But, be careful with how often you use them.

One of the dangers in using too many illustrations is that your listeners may become *dependent* on them. Getting a steady diet of sermons that are full of illustrations, funny stories, and interesting analogies can make it difficult for a person to sit through any kind of study or teaching that *doesn't* have the illustrations—and that would include your listener's own quiet times reading the Word. You don't want people to sit

---

[59] John MacArthur and Dr. Richard Mayhue, *Rediscovering Expository Preaching*, 248, 293–294.

[60] John Stott, *Between Two Worlds: The Challenge of Preaching Today*, 239.

down to read the Bible in the middle of the week and think, "It's just not as funny or interesting as when my pastor teaches it!"

I don't think a good sermon needs a lot of illustrations. If you speak plainly enough and explain the context of the passage and the historical background, your listeners can often understand what you are saying without an illustration. If you believe that something you are going to teach on will be a difficult concept for people to understand, then plan on sharing an illustration. But it need not be a long story.

Most of Jesus' illustrations are a paragraph or two in length. Many of the illustrations used by the New Testament authors are just short, simple analogies (e.g., "You are just a vapor that appears for a little while and then vanishes," James 4:14).

34. Don't repeatedly use your favorite illustrations.

"They will think the Word of God is boring,
when actually it is you!" –the author

When you seek to find an illustration for a point you want to make, there is the temptation to just use one you've used previously, rather than come up with a new one. There's a danger though in using recycled illustrations. Using the same illustrations over and over dulls the senses of the people you are teaching and tempts them to tune out. As soon as you launch into that story they have already heard once or twice over the past couple years, many of your listeners will think, "I already know this." The illustration ends up boring them.

The great danger in boring people with old worn out illustrations is that they will attach that feeling of boredom to

Word of God itself. They will think the Word of God is boring, when actually it is *you!*

It is good to remind people of God's truths but don't use the same moldy illustrations to do it. Get fresh illustrations for the timeless truths of God's Word. Here are some places to look for illustrations:

- **The Bible** (This is the best place to look. More on this in an upcoming point.)
- **Your life experience**
- **Books** (When I come across a good quote or illustration in a book, I make note of the page number in an alphabetical "Illustrations folder" I've created on my computer.)
- **The Biblical Illustrator** (This 56 volume collection of illustrations and quotes by Charles Spurgeon, Matthew Henry, Augustine, D. L. Moody, etc. is available as an add on in Bible study software programs.)
- **Bible.org/illustrations**
- **Biographies**
- **News stories**
- **Almanacs**
- **Guinness Book of World Records**
- **Other Bible Studies you've heard**
- ***Our Daily Bread*** (odb.org)

You can even create your own illustrations. Jesus did. You might start off your illustration or parable by saying something like, "*Imagine* one day you are driving your car down the road…" or "Let's *suppose* your friend comes over to your house one day really hungry…"

35. Use illustrations that actually serve a real purpose.

"We have to be ruthless in discarding the irrelevant…Irrelevant material will weaken the sermon's effect."[61] –John Stott

Illustrations can be big time-wasters and even distractions if not used carefully and sparingly. When you're considering using an illustration, ask yourself two questions:

1. **Does this illustration serve a real purpose? In other words, is it needed?**

2. **Does it help illustrate what is being said in the Scripture I am addressing?**

It is tempting to come across something you read or a scene in a heart-moving story and think, "I've got to share this with the people I teach!" Be careful. You don't have time to waste with stories that are not necessary. And you risk the danger of actually drawing attention *away* from the Word and the message God has for the people.

The well-known English preacher, F. B. Meyer, said this of a preacher he admired:

With merciless rigor he would *cut out every piece of needless rhetoric*, as the great artist struck the exquisitely painted chalice out of his picture of the Lord's Supper, because it

---

[61] John Stott, *Between Two Worlds: The Challenge of Preaching Today*, 228.

attracted attention which he meant to focus on the face of Christ.[62]

If your illustration is more memorable than the truth it is designed to illustrate, it could be considered a *distraction* rather than an illustration. In his book, *Between Two Worlds: The Challenge of Preaching Today*, John Stott writes:

> We have to be ruthless in discarding the irrelevant. This is easier said than done. During our hours of meditation numerous blessed thoughts and scintillating ideas may have occurred to us and been dutifully jotted down. It is tempting to drag them all in somehow. Resist the temptation! Irrelevant material will weaken the sermon's effect. It will come in handy some other time. We need the strength of mind to keep it till then.[63]

36. Don't betray someone's confidence for the sake of an illustration.

"He who goes about as a talebearer
reveals secrets, but he who is trustworthy
conceals a matter." (Prov. 11:13)

There are people in your life who have confided in you. They have confessed certain things to you. They have let you in on

---

[62] F. B. Meyer, *Jottings and Hints for Lay Preachers*, 17–18. Emphasis mine.
[63] Stott, *Between Two Worlds*, 228.

their fears and struggles. Don't refer to them and their struggles in your illustrations, especially by using their name:

- "I was talking to my friend Joe the other day about his struggle with (fill in the blank) and I got to thinking…"

- "There's a girl I know named Sarah who has a hard time loving the people that she works with…"

Rather than listening to how your story illustrates the Biblical text, many of your listeners will start thinking, "I can't believe Joe struggles with that!" They will start wondering, "What Sarah is he talking about? Is it the Sarah down the pew from me or perhaps the Sarah on the worship team? No. It's probably the Sarah who works at the church." And when you're done with the story, they are still wondering about it.

Obviously, an illustration like this does more harm than good. These kinds of illustrations lube the gossip mill and communicate to your listeners that you are not a person they should come to for prayer or counsel (Prov. 20:19). Who wants to seek counsel from a person who might turn around and refer to their situation in an illustration? So, don't betray someone's confidence for the sake of an illustration.

37. Avoid illustrations in which you end up being the hero.

"For we do not preach ourselves but
Christ Jesus." (2 Cor. 4:5)

It's fine to share stories from your own experience as illustrations—and I recommend that you do—but be careful to not share stories in such a way that *you* end up sounding like the hero of the story. The Psalmist said:

> Not to us, O LORD, not to us, but to *Thy name* give glory because of Thy lovingkindness, because of Thy truth (Ps. 115:1).

We want people to glorify the Lord, not us. We don't want people to leave our teachings thinking, "My pastor or Bible study leader is so great! How amazing that he would come to the rescue of that person or buy food for that poor family!"

Trumpet blowing was what the Pharisees did (Matt. 6:2). It should not be happening in today's pulpits. Solomon said, "Let another praise you, and not your own mouth; a stranger, and not your own lips" (Prov. 27:2). If good comes out of something you were involved in, and you feel compelled to share the story with your congregation, make sure you give the credit to the Lord (Isa. 10:15; Gal. 6:14).

The goal of our preaching is to point people to Jesus. Paul said, "We do not preach ourselves but Christ Jesus as Lord, and ourselves as your bond-servants for Jesus' sake" (2 Cor. 4:5). So, exalt Jesus and avoid illustrations in which you end up being the hero.

38. Use Biblical illustrations whenever possible.

"For whatever was written in earlier times was written for our instruction." (Rom. 15:4)

Although earlier I mentioned numerous sources for sermon illustrations, I really want to encourage you here to try to use

Biblical illustrations—illustrative material that comes right from the Bible—whenever you think an illustration would be helpful.

For example, let's suppose you are teaching through Ephesians 5 where you will be addressing Paul's admonition to "not get drunk with wine" (5:18). Rather than hunting around for a story in the newspaper that illustrates the dangers of drinking excessively, why not talk about Noah in Genesis 9 or Nabal and his foolish behavior in 1 Samuel 25?

Biblical illustrations do more than illustrate; they teach the Word because they *are* the Word (2 Tim. 3:16). The Bible tells us that, "these things happened to them as an example, and they were written for *our instruction*" (1 Cor. 10:11).

Talking about Noah or Nabal in an illustration will help expand a person's knowledge of the Bible. How many Christians today are really very familiar with who Nabal was? Maybe they would be if we used Biblical illustrations more often. I encourage you to do that.

To help you quickly find Biblical illustrations, I recommend the following books:

- *Nave's Topical Bible*
- *10,000 Illustrations from the Bible*
- *The Handbook of Bible Application*
- *Treasury of Scripture Knowledge*

Study Bibles, Bible commentaries and concordances can also be helpful.

THE PREPARATION
OF THE APPLICATION

39. Exhort those you are teaching to apply the Word to their own situation and to act.

"Preaching must have as its goal not only the impartation of truth, but also the transformation of life."[64] –Stephen Olford

As teachers, it is important to make clear to our listeners what God's Word *says* (observation) and explain what it *means*

---

[64] Stephen Olford and David Olford, *Anointed Expository Preaching*, 71.

(interpretation). But, we never want to leave it at that. The goal of observation and interpretation is *application*. James said, "Do not merely listen to the word, and so deceive yourselves. *Do* what it says" (James 1:22 NIV). God desires that we, and those we teach, live out His word.

Dwight Moody rightly acknowledged that, "God did not give us the Scriptures to increase our knowledge, but to change our lives."[65] The Lord told Joshua:

> This Book of the Law shall not depart from your mouth, but you shall meditate in it day and night, that you may observe to *do* according to all that is written in it. For *then* you will make your way prosperous, and *then* you will have good success (Joshua 1:8 NKJV).

Success for Joshua was intimately connected to him doing what God wanted him to do. And the same is true for Christians today. Jesus said, "If you know these things, blessed are you if you *do* them" (John 13:17 NKJV). So, as you are preparing your message, make sure to include in your notes places where you are going to encourage your listeners to apply God's Word to their own situation and act on it.

Now, discovering how a passage of Scripture actually applies to you and those you teach is not always easy. Here are some questions to ask as you study and prepare sermons that will help you extract possible applications.

- Are there commands to obey?
- Are there examples to follow?
- Are there errors or stumbling blocks to avoid?
- Are there sins to forsake?

---

[65] Cited in Earl D. Radmacher (ed.), *Celebrating the Word*, 47.

- Are there promises to claim?
- Are there principles to live by?
- What does this passage tell me about God or Jesus? [66]

Pondering the answers to these questions will help you discover some of the possible applications and how you might encourage your listeners to act.

40. Do not always keep the application for the end of the message.

"Teacher, what good thing shall I do…"
(Matt. 19:16)

Some teachers regularly save the application (the exhortation to act) for the end of their sermons. A popularly used sermon outline looks like this:

- Introduction
- Reading
- Explanation
- Illustration
- Application

I have followed this format and still do at times, but I encourage you to not feel locked in to this format. I say this especially for those of you who are, or will be teaching verse-by-verse through significant sections of Scripture, wherein the author deals with different subject matter. The format above tends to

---

[66] Adapted from Richard Mayhue, *How to Interpret the Bible for Yourself*, 64.

work better if you're teaching a topical message or covering a small section of Scripture.

One of the reasons I am not a big fan of this format is because I don't like holding back exhortations to act until the end of the message. When I read the Sermon on the Mount (Matt. 5–7), I see Jesus exhorting people to act every few verses:

- "Rejoice and be glad" (5:12)
- "Let your light shine" (5:16)
- "Leave your offering" (5:24)
- "Make friends quickly" (5:25)
- "Tear it out, and throw it from you" (5:29)
- "Make no oath at all" (5:34)
- "Let your statement be, 'Yes, yes'" (5:37)

These are just a few examples. If the greatest teacher who ever lived gave exhortations to act throughout His sermons, we are safe following in His footsteps.

41. Regularly include instruction, reminders and exhortation on the Holy Spirit.

"Not by might nor by power, but by my Spirit,"
says the Lord Almighty. (Zech. 4:6)

Christianity, as I have already noted, is not just a set of teachings to be understood and believed, it's a life that can be *lived out* in a way that is both pleasing and glorifying to God. But this life can only be lived out in this manner as followers of Christ walk in the power of the Holy Spirit by yielding to Him and allowing Him to work in their lives. Some Christians—no, *many* Christians (especially those younger in the faith)—don't realize this.

They realized they were sinners and in need of God's forgiveness. They heard the gospel. They trusted in Jesus to save them. They were born again and began attending a congregation of other believers. They heard sermons exhorting them to be holy, be patient, be kind, rejoice, serve the Lord, forgive their enemies, share the gospel, and so on. Eager to do well in their new adventure, they began striving to do and accomplish all that they were told to do. Unfortunately, many of these new believers (unaware of the Spirit's role in their lives) set out to follow Jesus' teachings:

- Trusting in their own will power and ingenuity
- Moving in their own energy and strength
- Leaning on their own intelligence
- Viewing God's instructions through pre-salvation lenses or experiences
- Employing past techniques learned in the world
- Practicing previous non-Christian religious disciplines
- Legalistically erecting non-Biblical restrictions to assist them in their desire to obey

And as they were doing one or more of the above, they appeared to be growing and spiritually healthy (they were at church twice a week or more). But a short way down the road of life, many of these people's determination to follow Jesus withered and died when weariness took its toll or they were unable to withstand the scorching headwinds of persecution, trials and temptations.

Overwhelmed with defeat, fatigue, and so on, they concluded that a joyful, victorious, fruitful Christian life is an impossible life to live. So, they gave up, threw in the towel and fell off the path of discipleship.[67]

I've seen it happen numerous times. You probably have too.

Well, these burned out believers came to the right conclusion—partially. The Christian life *is* an impossible life to live out—if you attempt to do it employing the methods above. But the Christian life *is* possible to live out—*if* you daily yield to and walk in the power of the Holy Spirit. When a believer is "filled with the Spirit" (Eph. 5:18), he will experience the work of the Spirit, who:

- Directs in the way of godliness (Ezk. 36:27)
- Delivers from sin (Gal. 5:16)
- Produces love, joy, peace, patience, kindness, goodness, faithfulness, gentleness, self-control (Gal. 5:22–23)
- Strengthens (Eph. 3:16; Col. 1:11)
- Comforts (Acts 9:31)
- Imparts hope (Rom. 15:13)
- Imparts the love of God (Rom. 5:3–5)
- Teaches (Jn. 14:26)
- Brings the Words of Christ to remembrance (Jn. 14:26)
- Guides (Jn. 16:13)
- Gives understanding (1 Cor. 2:12–13)
- Assists in prayer (Rom. 8:26–27; Jude 20)
- Delivers us from Satan (Eph. 6:10–11, 17–18)
- Enables us to witness to others (Acts 1:8; 1 Cor. 2:4)
- Gives courage (2 Tim. 1:7)
- Makes us Christlike (2 Cor. 3:17–18)

---

[67] I'm not suggesting they renounced Christ or lost their salvation, only that they fell away from fellowship and stopped moving forward in their spiritual maturity.

When believers don't understand some of these basic truths regarding the Holy Spirit, they are going to be hindered in their walks with the Lord. For Christians cannot experience the fullness of the fruit of the Spirit or the full work of the Spirit without daily surrendering to His influence in their lives. I agree with Spurgeon who said:

> There are many things that are desirable for the church of Christ, but one thing is absolutely needful; and this is the one thing, the power of the Holy Ghost in the midst of His people[68]...Without the Spirit of God we can do nothing. We are as ships without wind or chariots without steeds. Like branches without sap, we are withered. Like coals without fire, we are useless.[69]

Sadly though, many churches and preachers neglect speaking about Him. This is astonishing when you consider how important the work of the Spirit is in our lives and how often the Holy Spirit is talked about in the New Testament—the Book of Acts alone mentions the Holy Spirit about sixty times.[70] Could this be why so many churches are on the decline—dwindling in size, influence, fruitfulness, and so on? Have we neglected the Holy Spirit? Was Spurgeon right when he said, "If we do not honor the Holy Spirit, we cannot expect him to work with us. He will be grieved, and leave us to find out our helplessness"?[71] Was Francis Chan's popular book on the Holy

---

[68] Charles Spurgeon, "Converts and Their Confession of Faith," a sermon delivered on September 4, year not given.

[69] Charles Spurgeon, "A Revival Promise," in Warren Wiersbe, *Classic Sermons on Revival and Spiritual Renewal*, 46.

[70] Robert Gromacki, "The Holy Spirit: Who He Is, What He Does," in Charles Swindoll and Roy Zuck (eds.), *Understanding Christian Theology*, 478.

[71] Spurgeon in Wiersbe, *Classic Sermons on Revival*, 46.

Spirit a few years ago appropriately titled *Forgotten God*? I fear it was.

Well, fellow preachers, what shall we do?

First, determine that you yourself will not forget Him. Reacquaint yourself with what the Bible says about Him. Look up the verses in the list of Scriptures above and meditate on them. Read a good book dedicated to the person and work of the Holy Spirit. You may think you are sufficiently familiar with Him, but you may be surprised at how much you've forgotten if you read one or more of these books:

- *The Person and Work of the Holy Spirit* by R. A. Torrey
- *Living Water* by Chuck Smith
- *Forgotten God* by Francis Chan
- *The Holy Spirit* by John Walvoord
- *Mystery of the Holy Spirit* by A. W. Tozer

Second, regularly incorporate talk of the Holy Spirit and what He can do—and what He desires to do—into your teachings. Consider doing a topical series of teachings on the person and work of the Holy Spirit for the benefit of the people you teach. Consider teaching through the Book of Acts. I know of no better way to see people excited about walking in the power of the Spirit, than by teaching through that book. Whatever God leads you to do, make sure the Holy Spirit is not neglected or forgotten in your teachings.

THE PREPARATION OF THE CONCLUSION

42. Finish your teaching with a strong conclusion.

> *"The closing appeal should be the most carefully prepared. What is said last will linger longest... Let them be spoken as by one who pleads with the souls of men."[72] –F. B. Meyer*

When preparing a sermon, don't overlook how important it is to have a strong conclusion. Just like an athlete needs to be at

---

[72] F. B. Meyer, *Jottings and Hints for Lay Preachers*, 55.

his very best at the end of a race or a game, the preacher should strive to be at his best in the closing minutes.[73] There are a few purposes for a good conclusion:

- To review or summarize the content of your message
- To explain the sermon's application
- To exhort (or challenge) the listeners to obey the sermon's appeal
- To call for some sort of decision to mark the beginning of obedience
- To encourage, comfort, or in some other way build up the flock with the message[74]

You may choose to do a couple or all of these in your conclusion. However you decide to conclude, go out firing. The great preacher of old, G. Campbell Morgan, notes that:

> In the elaborated doctrinal part of Jonathan Edwards' sermon the great preacher was only getting his guns into position…in his applications [conclusions] he opened fire on the enemy. There are too many of us, I am afraid, who take so much time getting our guns into position that we have to finish without firing a shot. We say that we leave the truth to do its own work. We trust to the hearts and consciences of our hearers to apply it…this is a great and fatal mistake…A discourse which makes no spiritual or moral appeal or demand is not a sermon.[75]

---

[73] Richard Mayhue, *Rediscovering Expository Preaching*, 252.

[74] Ibid.

[75] G. Campbell Morgan, *Preaching*, 138–139.

I agree with Morgan. Closing a teaching by saying, "We will pick up again next week at verse 24" or "I trust that the Holy Spirit will show you how these things apply to your lives" is completely uninspiring.

Here are seven helpful suggestions to help you avoid a weak conclusion:

A. Do not add new material in the conclusion.

B. Make your conclusion clear and specific.

C. Let your conclusion reflect the demands of the passage you just preached.

D. Be direct and brief (no more than five minutes as a general rule).

If you value your reputation for truthfulness, don't say, "And now, in conclusion" or "Finally" and then go on for another six minutes before you say "And one other thing" before you finally say "And now before we depart." That will drive people crazy. Keep your promise.

E. When you begin a conclusion, avoid lapsing back into the message —*conclude.*

F. Answer the "What should I do?" question.

There are people who will be listening to you who need to change direction or their beliefs. Encourage them to do that.

G. Try to conclude with something for believers and nonbelievers.[76]

---

[76] These points were largely adapted from Richard Mayhue, *Rediscovering Expository Preaching*, 253.

THE PREACHER'S REST

43. Sleep well the night before you teach.

"He gives to His beloved sleep." (Ps. 127:2 ESV)

Many a teacher of God's Word has found himself up late studying and preparing for a sermon. And there are times when family needs, ministry demands and so on, end up requiring that.

Back in the late nineteen nineties, I was the pastor of the college ministry at Calvary Chapel in Vista, California. As is the case oftentimes with assistant pastors, I was buried with ministry responsibilities. In addition to leading the college group, I was on call for walk-in counseling needs, the director of and an instructor at our School of Ministry, the young married couples pastor, the sound man for church and school activities, the graphic artist, and the janitor of our K-12 school every Wednesday.

With all of that on my plate, I found it impossible to get any studying done for the regular Sunday morning college gathering until my day off on Saturdays. This regularly required that I drive over to my office at the church (where my library of books and only computer were) and stay up until 2:00 or 3:00 AM on Sunday morning studying for that morning's teaching.

My good friend, Scott Cunningham, the high school pastor at the time, was in the same predicament. So we would bump into each other every Saturday afternoon at the church to study. Around midnight every Saturday, when we were keeling over from exhaustion and feeling like we could go on no longer, we would take a short break and walk over to the nearby 7–11 for a cup of coffee. On the way to what we wished was a Starbucks, we would discuss the progress of our preparations and console ourselves with reminders that Paul said his ministry involved "many sleepless nights" (2 Cor. 11:27). When we got back to the church, we'd work for another two or three hours typing out our notes until we could go on no longer. Despite the sermon notes hardly being what we wanted them to be, we would agree they'd have to suffice as we locked up the doors and headed to our homes.

After sleeping for two or three hours, I'd return to open the church building at 6:00 AM, set up the stage for the worship team—I was the sound man you recall—and do a sound check, even as I frantically read through my notes at the soundboard.

When 9:15 rolled around, I would hand off the sound responsibilities, stumble over to the college gathering and do my best to open my Bible and share my nocturnal discoveries with the bright-eyed men and women who thought staying out at Denny's until eleven o'clock the night before was late.

I share this with you to assure you that I can relate with those who are pressed into late night sermon preparation. But friends, as I'm sure you'd agree, standing before God's people with droopy eyelids and slurred speech is not the ideal way to deliver a sermon. God's grace saw me through many groggy sermons during those years doing that, but I was rarely at my best apart from a good night of sleep. And I think that holds true for most preachers.

So, if at all possible, I encourage you to prioritize your schedule and study time so that you're regularly done with your sermon preparation early enough to get a good night of sleep the night before you teach.

If you are in the position of delegating ministry responsibilities to a staff of other servants and teachers, make sure you give them enough time to adequately study and prepare for their sermons. They shouldn't have to neglect their families every week on their day off to study and prepare for a teaching.

THE PREACHING OF THE SERMON

44. Be mindful that you preach in the sight of God.

"He who formed the eye, does He not see?"
(Ps. 94:9)

One of the truths that has served as a great motivation to me in my efforts to handle God's Word properly and preach it with excellence is found in something Paul said to the Corinthians: "For we are not like many, peddling the word of God, but as from sincerity, but as from God, we speak in Christ *in the sight of God*" (2 Cor. 2:17).

Paul knew very well that everything he said and taught others was taking place in the sight of God. The Bible says, "There is no creature hidden from His sight, but all things are open and laid bare to the eyes of Him with whom we have to do" (Heb. 4:13). This should motivate all who handle God's Word to do so carefully and faithfully!

Not only is everything you speak happening in the sight of God, one day you will stand before Him to have your life and ministry evaluated.

> For we must all appear before the judgment seat of Christ, so that each one may be recompensed for his deeds in the body, according to what he has done, whether good or bad (2 Cor. 5:10).

For the unsaved, it will be a judgment of *condemnation*. For believers, it will be a judgment of *evaluation* where:

> Fire will reveal what kind of work each builder has done. The fire will show if a person's work has any value. If the work survives, that builder will receive a reward. But if the work is burned up, the builder will suffer great loss. The builder will be saved, but like someone barely escaping through a wall of flames (1 Cor. 3:13–15 NLT).

Think of that. One day, your work, your ministry, your preaching is going to be evaluated by the Lord. Let that move you to handle God's Word reverently and to preach His truth with great care.

45. Preach that God may be glorified.

"Whatever you do, do all to the glory of God."
(1 Cor. 10:31 NKJV)

In his first epistle, Peter wrote:

> As each one has received a gift, minister it to one another, as good stewards of the manifold grace of God. If anyone speaks, let him speak as the oracles of God. If anyone ministers, let him do it as with the ability which God supplies, [Why?] that in all things *God* may be glorified through Jesus Christ, to whom belong the glory and the dominion forever and ever. Amen (1 Pet. 4:10–11 NKJV).

This must be one of our supreme goals when we preach—preaching to bring God glory. We bring God glory in our preaching by leading others to praise Him and cherish elevated, reverential, proper thoughts about Him and His Word.[77]

And since the goal is seeing that *God* gets the glory in and through our preaching, there is never a time for boasting or magnifying ourselves in the pulpit (Jer. 9:23–24). The preacher must remember that everything—his eloquence, reason, voice, imagination, good health, all of his abilities, his entire life—is all the gift and creation of God. This is to say nothing about the ground the church sits on, the wood making up the pulpit, etc. All of these things were created through Him and *for* Him (Col. 1:16). Where is there room for boasting, drawing attention to ourselves or robbing God of the glory that belongs to

---

[77] See Albert Barnes, *Barnes' Notes on the Bible*, 1 Corinthians 10:31.

Him? There is none. Jesus said, "apart from Me you can do nothing" (John 15:5).

Knowing this, Paul said, "May it never be that I would boast, except in the cross of our Lord Jesus Christ, through which the world has been crucified to me, and I to the world" (Gal. 6:14). In his letter to the Ephesians and elsewhere Paul even demotes himself: "To me, the very *least* of all saints, this grace was given, to preach to the Gentiles the unfathomable riches of Christ" (Eph. 3:8). Humility should mark the life of every disciple of Christ—how much more those who teach God's Word?

Recalling a time when he was about to teach, John Jowett, the man who assumed G. Campbell Morgan's role at Westminster Chapel, says someone prayed for him, "O Lord, we thank Thee for our brother. Now blot him out. Reveal Thy glory to us in such blazing splendor that he shall be forgotten."[78]

What a great prayer! Oh, that more people would leave our sermons forgetting about us because their hearts and minds are overflowing with praise and elevated, reverential thoughts about our glorious God!

46. Keep your comments brief when you step up to the pulpit.

"General comments about the weather, the congregation, the music, special guests, and even the announcements...For goodness' sake, start preaching!"[79] *–Warren Wiersbe*

---

[78] John Henry Jowett, *The Preacher, His Life and Work*, 151.
[79] Warren Wiersbe and David Wiersbe, *The Elements of Preaching*, 75–76.

When you approach the pulpit to teach, I encourage you to not get bogged down with peripheral matters. Make a beeline as quickly as possible to the teaching. The beloved, veteran preacher, Warren Wiersbe, explains:

> A preacher is like a man who hears a call for help and drops everything to run to the rescue...when he spends five or ten minutes getting into his sermon, he is like a man pausing to visit an art gallery before diving into the ocean to save the drowning swimmer.[80]

Some of the chief time wasters preachers get entangled with, according to Wiersbe, are:

A. General comments about the weather, the congregation, the music, special guests, and even the announcements

Wiersbe says, "If you feel constrained to discuss the inanities, do so before you stand up to preach. But keep in mind that every minute you waste early in the service will rob you of preaching time."[81]

B. Comments about the sermon itself

Wiersbe says, "Some preachers don't seem to understand that we don't want to hear *about* the sermon; we want to hear the sermon...On more than one occasion, we have found ourselves repressing the strong desire to shout, 'For goodness' sake, start preaching! What reverend sir, are you driving at?'"[82]

---

[80] Ibid., 75.

[81] Ibid., 76.

[82] Ibid., 76, 75.

47. Don't feel it necessary, as you begin your teaching, to always review your previous message.

"Now, you'll recall that last week…"
–the preacher

Reviewing previously covered territory can be helpful to your listeners but if you do that every week, or if you go on reviewing too long, people are going to tune out. Warren Wiersbe says:

> Here sits a man with a broken heart and a problem-filled life. He came to church hoping to get some help from God's Word. The choir has sung and the song helped prepare him for the message. The preacher opens his mouth and says, "Now, you'll recall that last week—or was it two weeks ago—we discussed the first six verses of this chapter." Instantly our needy visitor says, "Well, I should have come last week…but maybe there's still hope." Instead of the preacher getting to the point, he tries to summarize three weeks of preaching; and by that time, our friend isn't listening anymore.[83]

If you are going to review previous material, keep it concise. You might say something like, "In last week's study we looked at the events surrounding Jesus' resurrection. In today's study we are going to consider the events that followed the resurrection." If people want to get a point-by-point recap of a previous teaching, they can go to the church website and listen, get the CD, get it via podcast, etc.

---

[83] Ibid., 76.

48. Preach the Word with confidence and authority.

"Therefore having such a hope, we use great boldness in our speech." (2 Cor. 3:12)

The Bible is God's authoritative Word to man. Because this is the case, proclaim it confidently—not with *self*-confidence, but with the confidence that as you speak forth God's Word, the King is speaking. Charles Spurgeon said:

> I recollect a young man going into a pulpit to address a congregation, and he began by saying that he hoped they would pardon his youth and forgive his impertinence in coming to speak to them. Some foolish old gentleman said, "How humble that young man is to talk like that!" But another said, "What a dishonor to his Lord and Master! If God sent him with a message to those people, what does it matter whether he is young or old? Such mock modesty as that is out of place in the pulpit." I think that second man was right. A true minister of the gospel is an ambassador for Christ, and do our ambassadors go to foreign courts with apologies or carrying messages from their sovereign?[84]

Spurgeon is right. Our countries' ambassadors don't go out apologizing unless their king or country has done something wrong. Our heavenly King has done nothing wrong. Ever. Therefore, there is no need to be apologetic in the pulpit. Paul said, "We are ambassadors for Christ, as though *God* were

---

[84] Charles Spurgeon, "Preaching Christ Crucified," a sermon delivered on August 23, 1863.

pleading through us" (2 Cor. 5:20 NKJV). When you speak forth God's Word, it is as though God is speaking through you. Because that is the case, a herald for the King should not say things like:

- "I hate to say this, but _____ is sinful."
- "If Jesus's words here offend you, I'm sorry."
- "I didn't say that; God said it!"[85]

The herald of God's Word should declare what God has to say unashamedly, with authority and conviction.

In his second epistle to Timothy, Paul told him to "*Preach the Word!*" (2 Tim. 4:2 NKJV). Kenneth Wuest, the well-known Greek scholar, says the word *preach* here:

> was used of the imperial herald, spokesman of Caesar Augustus, who when entering a town as a representative of the Emperor would make a public proclamation of the Emperor's message with such formality, gravity, and authority as must be heeded and obeyed. A full translation, therefore, of Paul's exhortation [in 2 Tim. 4:2] is: "Make a public proclamation of the Word with such formality, gravity, and authority as must be heeded and obeyed."[86]

When you stand up to teach the Scriptures, you are a messenger—not for Caesar, but for the King of the Caesars—the King of kings. If you've interpreted the passage carefully, then you can speak authoritatively and boldly because the message is not *yours*. It's the King's! And not only *can* you speak this way,

---

85 …with sort of an ashamed tone that He did.

86 Kenneth Wuest, *The New Testament: An Expanded Translation*, ix.

you *should* speak this way. Paul told Titus, and us by implication, "These things speak and exhort and reprove with all *authority*...I want you to speak *confidently*" (Tit. 2:15, 3:8). This does not mean yelling or shaking your fist. Bryan Chapell points out that:

> A pastor confident of the Bible's truth is able to preach with great *force* or with great *gentleness* and still speak with authority...The authority of the Word enables us to say the most challenging things to any person without apology, but that same authority lets us speak tenderly without compromising strength.[87]

Authority was one of things that impressed those who heard Jesus teach. Matthew tells us "when Jesus had ended these sayings [the sermon on the mount], that the people were astonished at His teaching, for He taught them as one having *authority*, and not as the scribes (Matt. 7:28–29 NKJV)." The scribes were always quoting the opinions of the rabbis.[88] How frustrating it must have been to listen to them teach. I imagine some of their listeners wanted to stand up and say, "What does *God* have to say about the matter?" Jesus came along and told the people, *'This is the way it is in the Kingdom of God'* (e.g., Mark 4:26, 10:14, 23–24). The people were astonished by that!

So, research the passage, interpret the passage correctly, pray for boldness (Acts 4:29–31; Eph. 6:19) and then emulate Jesus. Speak with authority. *Preach* the Word.

---

[87] Bryan Chapell, *Christ-Centered Preaching*, 89. Emphasis mine.

[88] See John Gill's comments on Matthew 7:29 in *John Gill's Exposition of the Bible*. This commentary is available online at http://www.biblestudy tools.com/commentaries/gills-exposition-of-the-bible.

49. Speak directly to the people you are teaching, not neglecting to use the word "You."

"There must be a directness in our addresses.
Each sermon must say in the words of Nathan,
'Thou art the man.'"[89] –F. B. Meyer

I remember early on as a young teacher, neglecting to speak *directly* to my listeners. I continually said things like:

- "As Christians, *we* need to be careful how *we* talk about others"
- "*We* need to remember that God loves *us*."
- "*Believers* need to accept…"
- "Some of *us* need to admit that *we* are guilty."

I wanted those listening to understand that I knew I was one of them—no better than them—and in need of the same teaching they were receiving. My intentions were good, but I believe now that I was doing them a disservice. There *are* times for speaking this way and even times when we *should* speak this way, but I think it is far better for the listener to feel as though the speaker (you) means *him* by saying:

- "The Bible says *you* must be careful how you speak about others."
- "God loves *you*."

---

[89] F. B. Meyer, *Jottings and Hints for Lay Preachers*, 71.

If you look at the messages of the preachers in the Bible, it is amazing to note the lack of the word *we*. Throughout the Scriptures when one of God's heralds vocally addressed a group of people, he spoke very directly. The examples abound. Consider Peter's sermon in Acts chapter 2. Over and over again, Peter said things like:

- "*You* men of Israel"
- "*You* yourselves"
- "*You*...did crucify"

Consider Jesus' directness in the sermon on the mount: "*You* are the light of the world...*Your* Father knows what *you* need, before *you* ask Him...Beware of the false prophets, who come to *you* in sheep's clothing" (Matt. 5:14, 6:8, 7:15).

John the Baptist said, "Do not suppose that *you* can say to *yourselves*, 'We have Abraham for our father' (Matt. 3:9)...be content with *your* wages" (Luke 3:14). The Old Testament prophets spoke this way also. So...

Rather than say:	There are times when it would be better to say:
• "**We** can't serve God and money."	• "**You** can't serve God and money."
• "God desires that **we** rejoice in the Lord."	• "God desires that **you** rejoice in the Lord."
• "**Some of us** are struggling with anxiousness."	• "Perhaps some of **you** are struggling with anxiousness."

- "The Bible says **we** need to flee sexual immorality."

- "The Bible says **you** need to flee sexual immorality."

The people in your congregation need to know the message has something for them *personally*—that God has something to say to *them*. Speak to them that way.

50. Preach with passion.

"Preaching is theology coming through a man who is on fire…A man who can speak about these things dispassionately has no right whatsoever to be in a pulpit."[90] *–Martyn Lloyd-Jones*

Charles Spurgeon told the story long ago of a man traveling in the dark of night by foot. He was headed toward a bridge that had collapsed into a storm-swollen, raging river. Someone attempted to stop him from going further saying that he had heard the bridge might be out. There was no conviction in the man's voice, so the traveler continued walking supposing the man to be in error. Then another man came along and said:

"Sir, sir, the bridge is gone!"

"Oh, yes," replied the traveler. "Someone told me that story a little while ago, but I'm sure it is an idle tale."

"Oh, it is true!" exclaimed the other. "I barely escaped being carried away with it myself. You must not go on." In the excitement of his feelings, he grasped the traveler by the hands, by the arms, by the clothes.

---

[90] Martyn Lloyd-Jones, *Preaching and Preachers*, 97.

Convinced by the earnest voice, the earnest eyes, the earnest gestures, the traveler turned back and was saved. So it is only through a burning zeal for the salvation of the lost—a zeal glowing in the heart and flashing out in look and action and utterance—that the confidence of unbelief can be overcome and the heedless travelers of the broad way won to the path of life and happiness.[91]

I agree with Spurgeon—our preaching should come across with earnestness, zeal, and passion. This doesn't mean we are marching around the pulpit with large gestures and raised voices. But we should seek to be the kind of people who are genuinely enthusiastic about the things of God—so much so, that when we teach others, our conviction and passion are evident.

In a sermon he delivered in 1856, at New Park Street Chapel, in England, Spurgeon said:

If ministers of the gospel were more hearty in their work of preaching; if…they would preach the Word of God, and preach it *as if they were pleading for their own lives*, ah! then, my brethren, we might expect great success; but we cannot expect it while we go about our work in a half-hearted way, and have not that zeal, that earnestness, that deep purpose which characterized those men of old.[92]

If we are spiritually drowsy in the pulpit, we are going to have a difficult time convincing our listeners that what we say is

---

[91] Charles Spurgeon, *Feathers for Arrows: Illustrations for Preachers and Teachers From My Notebook*, 267–268.

[92] Charles Spurgeon, "Gospel Missions," a sermon delivered on April 27, 1856. Emphasis mine.

important or even worth listening to. In 1656, the Puritan pastor, Richard Baxter, wrote:

> How few ministers preach with all their might or speak of everlasting joy or torment with conviction. Instead, we speak so drowsily or gently that sleeping sinners cannot hear.[93]

Sleeping sinners (and I might add some saints) think our lack of conviction—our lack of passion—is because we are really not *convinced* of the truthfulness of what we preach. And if *we* are not convinced, why should *they* be? Spurgeon said:

> If you want to win souls for Christ, feel a solemn alarm about them. You cannot make them feel if you do not feel yourself. Believe their danger, believe their helplessness, believe that only Christ can save them, and talk to them as if you meant it. The Holy Spirit will move them by first moving you. If you can rest without their being saved, they will rest, too. But if you are filled with an agony for them, if you cannot bear that they should be lost, you will soon find that they are uneasy, too. I hope you will get into such a state that you will dream about your child or your hearer perishing for lack of Christ, and start up at once and begin to cry, "Oh God, give me converts or I will die." Then you will have converts.[94]

---

[93] Cited by Wallace Benn, "Preaching with a Pastor's Heart: Richard Baxter's *The Reformed Pastor*," in *Preach the Word: Essays on Expository Preaching in Honor of R. Kent Hughes*, 138.

[94] Charles Spurgeon, "Conversions Desired," a sermon delivered on March 5, 1876.

Spurgeon says, "begin to cry" out. That is the cure for passion-less preaching. That is the remedy for the preacher who realizes he's lacking zeal and earnestness for the things of God.

Will not God answer the prayer of the person who runs to His throne of grace and fervently cries out for God to stir his heart, revive him, change him and give him as F. B. Meyer said, "a passion for His glory, a passion for the souls of men...that [his] words may glow and burn like coals"?[95] Surely, He will! Those are the very kinds of prayers you can be certain God will answer in the affirmative (1 Jn. 5:14–15).

51. Preach in the present tense.

"God is faithful." (1 Cor. 10:13)

One of the goals in preaching is to bring the truths of Scripture in to the here and now. In their book, *The Elements of Preaching*, Warren and David Wiersbe said:

> Nobody goes to church to find out what happened to the Jebusites. A sermon that lingers in the past tense is not really a sermon at all: it is either a Bible story or a lecture. We *live* in the present tense and we need to hear what God has to say to us *today*.[96]

So, instead of emphasizing the following as a main point:

- God *was* faithful to the children of Israel in the wilderness

---

[95] F. B. Meyer, *Jots and Hints for Lay Preachers*, 116–117.

[96] Warren Wiersbe and David Wiersbe, *The Elements of Preaching*, 66.

...bring that truth into the present. It is true that God *was* faithful, but it would be better to emphasize:

- God *is* faithful
- God *will be* faithful

Rather than this for a main point:

- God forgave them when they repented

...*consider this:*

- God forgives repentant sinners

Rather than this for a main point:

- Compromise led Solomon to greater disobedience

...*consider this:*

- Compromise often leads to greater disobedience

Do you see the difference? We're bringing the truths of the Bible into the here and now. It is good and even necessary to point out facts about the *past* (Rom. 15:4, 1 Cor. 10:11), but you can excel as a teacher if you will hammer home to your listeners the *present* realities.

The Bible tells us that God is the same today as He was in the days of the Old Testament (Heb. 13:8). The principles and truths of the Bible are timeless. God says, "I am the LORD, I do not change" (Mal. 3:6). Anything that was true about the nature and character of God in the Bible is true of Him in our day and age also. Remind your listeners of that.

52. Aim to speak clear enough so as to not be misunderstood.

"A preacher ought so to preach, that when the sermon is ended, the congregation shall disperse saying, 'The preacher said this.'"[97] *–Martin Luther*

The apostle Paul asked the Colossian believers to pray for him so that when he proclaimed God's truth to others he would "make it *clear*, which is how I ought to speak" (Col. 4:4 ESV). Clarity, of course, is of utmost importance and wise speakers everywhere realize this. They aim to speak clear enough to be understood. But I encourage you to aim even higher. Seek to speak so clearly that there is little to no chance you will be *misunderstood*.

This is one reason I encourage you to consider writing out most of what you intend to say at the pulpit. Doing this will allow you to go back over your notes *before* you teach and make sure that:

- What you are going to say is clear
- You are not going to lose people
- Your thoughts flow well
- You are not going to use words or phrases that the average person won't understand

Remember, your goal is not to impress people with your grasp of the English language—or the Greek or Hebrew for that matter. Your goal is to express the truths of God's Word so clearly and plainly that your listeners can follow you and

---

[97] Cited in G. Campbell Morgan, *Preaching*, 49.

understand what God's Word says and means. God forbid that people leave our teachings wishing they had brought their dictionaries.

I agree with Bryan Chapell who says the "true mark of pastoral genius" is "to say profound things simply."[98] Charles Spurgeon said:

> God is my witness—I have eschewed every idea of trying to be eloquent or oratorical in my preaching! I care nothing whatever about the gaudy show of speechmaking. I only want to tell you these truths of God in unvarnished speech.[99] ...The use of six-syllabled jaw-breaking words is simply a most ludicrous vanity.[100]

If you do use an occasional "big" word (e.g., soteriology, eschatology, atonement, vicarious, premillennial, theophany, justification), think about supplying a brief definition in the same sentence so that people know what you're saying. Here are three quick examples:

A. "One of my favorite books on *eschatology* is by Dwight Pentecost..."

New believers—and many older believers—are going to think, "What is he talking about?"

Alternative: "One of my favorite books on eschatology, or the study of end-time Bible prophecy, is..."

---

[98] Bryan Chapell, *Christ-Centered Preaching*, 123.

[99] Charles Spurgeon, "Simple Fact and Simple Faith," a sermon published on January 18, 1917. No teaching date given.

[100] *The Quotable Spurgeon*, QuickVerse.

By adding a short definition after the word *eschatology*, you've defined the word mid-sentence and ensured that everyone is going to be able to continue listening with understanding.

B. "I think a *plausible* explanation for this apparent contradiction in the Bible is…"

The word "plausible" is going to go over the heads of a chunk of your congregation. So, if you really want to use the word *plausible*, you might say:

Alternative: "I think a plausible, *or probable*, explanation for this…"

C. "*Ostensibly*, Jesus' reason for eating in front of the disciples reflects His desire to show He is not a *disembodied* ghost…"

Ostensibly? Disembodied? *Really?*

Alternative: "It appears that Jesus' reason for eating in front of the disciples was to demonstrate to them that He had really conquered death in the same body that had been crucified.

Now, these examples raise a question. If words like *ostensibly, plausible,* or *eschatology* are going to go over the heads of a good percentage of the congregation, why use them?—especially if there are more commonly understood words or phrases that will suffice. That's a question you, as a teacher, need to ponder. I *can* see the benefit in helping the congregation expand their vocabulary but God forbid we lose them in the process or do any of this trying to impress them.

The best teachers follow in the footsteps of Jesus and "the common people heard Him gladly" (Mk. 12:37 NKJV). I pray the same will be said of you and me. May God give us wisdom and humility when choosing our words (Ecc. 12:9–11).

53. Preach apologetically; contend for the faith.

"Contend earnestly for the faith which was once for all delivered to the saints." (Jude 3)

One of the goals in teaching, as you already know, is to exhort your listeners with sound doctrine, explaining to them what is *right*. But another goal is refuting those who are *wrong*, those who contradict sound doctrine. In fact, being able to do so is a requirement for pastors. Paul told Timothy:

> For the overseer *must be*…holding fast the faithful word which is in accordance with the teaching, so that he will be able both to *exhort* in sound doctrine and to *refute* those who contradict (Titus 1:7–9).

Faithfully teaching God's Word in an expository way will go a long way in helping your listeners understand and walk in sound doctrine. But they also need help seeing the errors of those who contradict sound doctrine.

As you are aware, there are a variety of groups that offer alternative, aberrant, and even heretical views of certain Scriptures (e.g., Jehovah's Witnesses, Mormons, Muslims, homosexuals, emerging church leaders, word of faith teachers). The wise shepherd who is concerned for the wellbeing of the flock will be on the lookout for opportunities to lovingly "refute those who contradict" sound doctrine.

For example, when he comes to a verse that affirms the deity of Christ (e.g., John 8:58, 20:28), rather than just affirming what it says, he might also take the time to refute the typical Jehovah Witness response to the verse. When teaching through a passage that is commonly attacked by critics, such as God's command to destroy the Canaanite cities (Deut. 20:16–18; Josh. 6:21), he might spend some time responding to the critics' objections. This is preaching apologetically. This is contending for the faith (Jude 3).

Your listeners should not be getting apologetics once or twice a year when a guest speaker is brought in. They should be getting this kind of help throughout the year.

To help you contend for the faith in the pulpit, I encourage you to keep a copy of *The Big Book of Bible Difficulties* (previously titled *When Critics Ask*) by Norman Geisler and Thomas Howe on your desk. It addresses in book-by-book order, just about every passage in the Bible that the cults twist or that critics scoff at. Another helpful book is *Commonly Misunderstood Bible Verses* by Ron Rhodes.[101]

54. Speak to the current issues of the day.

"Failure to show the bearing of the gospel on such issues is merely to trumpet that there is no bearing."[102] –D. A. Carson.

---

[101] Both of these books are available at AlwaysBeReady.com.

[102] D. A. Carson, "Challenges for the Twenty-first-century Pulpit," *Preach the Word: Essays on Expository Preaching in Honor of R. Kent Hughes*, 187.

As you teach through the Word, look for opportunities to show what bearing God's Word has on many of the current issues of the day:

- Pornography
- Islam
- Abortion
- Homosexuality
- Moral relativism
- Religious pluralism
- Middle East tensions
- Environmental issues
- War
- Euthanasia
- Cloning
- Stem Cell Research
- Capital Punishment
- Substance Abuse
- Same Sex Marriage

Although the Bible doesn't mention some of these issues by name, there are verses that speak to these issues. And these are issues that people are confronted with every day in the culture and on the news. Many people want to know what the Bible has to say about these issues. So, as the opportunity presents itself, mention these matters and show what the Bible would have God's people to think about these issues. I agree with D. A. Carson, who writes:

> Christian preachers are not authorized to duck important issues. At the same time, these issues must not determine his message. Yet failure to show the bearing of the gospel on such issues is merely to trumpet that there is no bearing.

Our task, then, is to be expositors of the Word of God yet to exercise that ministry in the time and place where God has providentially placed us.[103]

Two books that will help you speak about these issues from a Biblical perspective are *Christian Ethics: Options and Issues* by Norman Geisler and a similar but shorter book called *Love Your Neighbor: Thinking Wisely About Right and Wrong* by Norman Geisler and Ryan Snuffer.[104]

55. Preach the gospel and keep it Biblical.

"I always feel that I have not done my duty as a preacher of the gospel if I go out of this pulpit without having clearly set before sinners the way of salvation."[105] –Charles Spurgeon

Jesus said, "Go into all the world and preach the gospel to all creation" (Mk. 16:15). The fact that sinful, rebellious human beings can:

- Be delivered from the power of sin and death
- Be forgiven by God
- Escape eternity in Hell
- Be declared righteous in God's sight
- Be reconciled to God
- Enjoy everlasting life with God, the angels and redeemed

---

[103] Ibid.

[104] Both of these books are available at AlwaysBeReady.com.

[105] Charles Spurgeon, "Migratory Birds," a sermon delivered on August 28, 1870.

...because of Jesus' death and resurrection on our behalf is the greatest news the world could ever hear.

How is it then, at the pulpit—possibly blessed by the presence of even one nonbeliever—that we could neglect to share that good news with them? And yet it happens. I've been guilty.

Seeing that we never know when a nonbeliever may visit our home fellowship, class, conference, or Sunday service, I believe every preacher should think through how he's going to include the gospel in his message before he teaches.[106]

When you *do* share the gospel, make sure that what you say is Biblical. That is, be sure every phrase you utter can be backed up with Scripture. The Bible has a strong warning for anyone who distorts the gospel (Gal. 1:8). In light of this warning, we do not want to tamper with the gospel!

Rob Bell—a highly controversial and I believe heretical teacher—has great crowds of churchgoers flocking to his teachings and buying his videos.[107] Rob was asked in *Christianity Today* how he would explain the gospel on Twitter. Here was Rob's response:

> I would say that history is headed somewhere. The thousands of little ways in which you are tempted to believe that hope might actually be a legitimate response to the insanity of the world actually can be trusted. And the Christian story is that a tomb is empty, and a movement has actually begun that has been present in a sense all

---

[106] I said earlier in the book that if you are teaching a small group and are confident that everyone is saved, then giving a detailed explanation of the gospel every week is not necessary. If there is someone new there though and you are unsure of his or her spiritual condition, make sure to share the gospel. He may never have another chance to hear it.

[107] See the section on the "Emerging Church" at AlwaysBeReady.com for more on Rob Bell.

along in creation. And all those times when your cynicism was at odds with an impulse within you that said that this little thing might be about something bigger—those tiny little slivers may in fact be connected to something really, really big.[108]

Hunh? I had to read that four or five times to try and figure out what he was saying. This is not the gospel. Where's the mention of the cross, faith in Christ, repentance, forgiveness of sins, everlasting life, etc.? This is not the gospel the disciples preached. This is the gospel according to Rob Bell. Contrast Bell's gospel with Scriptures like:

- John 3:16
- Acts 16:30–31
- Romans 5:8, 10:9–10
- 1 Corinthians 15:1–4
- 1 Timothy 1:15

Now, I'm sure most of you reading this book would say, "Charlie, I would never present a gospel like Rob Bell's quote above." I commend you for that. But I also want to encourage you to avoid popular clichés that sound more Scriptural than Bell's gospel—but nevertheless, are not the gospel either. I'm talking about clichés like:

Cliché No. 1:
"Give your heart (or life) to Christ and be saved."

---

[108] From interview with Mark Galli in *Christianity Today*. http://www.christianitytoday.com/ct/article_print.html?id=81195.

There's a serious problem with this cliché. It is often understood by nonbelievers to be requiring more than what the Bible actually requires for a person to be saved.

The Bible says we are "justified as a *gift* by His grace" (Rom. 3:24) and that everlasting life is a "*free gift*" (Rom. 6:23) laid hold of by *faith* in Christ (Jn. 3:16, 36; Rom. 5:1; 1 Jn. 5:13). I don't want a nonbeliever to think he has to *give* his heart, life, or anything to Christ in order to be saved.

What if a friend called you up and said, "I have a free gift for you. I'd like to bring it over to you."

So, you agree and say, "Thank you! Come on over."

Your friend drives over and has a big box with a red bow on it. He holds it out to you. As soon as you reach out to receive it, he yanks it back and says, "If you'd like the gift, you need to give me your heart or your life!"

What would you think? Would that be a "free gift?" No. That's a gift with a huge price tag. The *heart*, Biblically speaking, is the core of who a person is, the center not only of spiritual activity, but of all the operations of human life.[109] A *life* is widely understood to mean a person's entire life—all his time, talents, dreams, desires, etc. When we tell a person, "Give your heart (or life) to Christ and be saved," we are putting a price tag on salvation. That is not the gospel. That is not good news. I can't find any verses that require a person to give *anything* to the Lord in order to be saved. A "free gift" (Rom. 6:23) is free, is it not? Charles Spurgeon agreed that this popular cliché is problematic. He said:

> I am continually hearing, from converts and others, the expression, "I gave my heart to Christ," as a description of

---

[109] This is a widely accepted, Biblical definition of *heart*. See http://www.biblestudytools.com/dictionaries/eastons-bible-dictionary/heart.html.

conversion. Now I do not find fault with that expression, for we must give our hearts to Christ—but very seriously let me say that I am afraid that that phrase will do much mischief unless it is well guarded and looked after. The gospel is not, "Give your hearts to Christ, and you shall be saved." The gospel is, "Believe on the Lord Jesus Christ"— that is, *trust* Him—"and you shall be saved." When you do that, you will be sure to give Him your heart, by-and-by, if not at once. Salvation is not by your giving anything to Christ, but by Christ giving something to you! I am glad that you have given your heart to Christ—but have you learned, first, this lesson—that He gave His heart for you? We do not find salvation by giving Christ anything! That is the fruit of it, but salvation comes by Christ giving us something—did I say something—by Christ giving us *everything!* By His giving us Himself![110]

Spurgeon wanted to keep the gospel he preached Scriptural. He goes right back to the Bible and says, *'This is actually what the Scriptures say: "Believe on the Lord..."'* He was determined to keep the gospel purely Biblical; he didn't want to tamper with it one bit. Spurgeon said:

I am content to live and to die as the mere repeater of Scriptural teaching; as a person who has thought out nothing, and invented nothing, as one who never thought invention to be any part of his calling; but who concluded that he was to take the message from the lips of God to the best of his ability, and simply to be a mouth for God

---

[110] Charles Spurgeon, "Sychar's Sinner Saved," a sermon delivered on April 13, 1890.

to the people, mourning much that anything of his own should come between.[111]

Amen to that. Heralds for kings are to be *messengers* not *editors*.

Cliché No. 2:
"To be saved you need to invite Jesus into your heart."

This is another widely used cliché that needs to be abandoned. Here's why.

First, it is unscriptural. There are no verses in the Scriptures that tell a person to do this. The verse often quoted in conjunction with it is Revelation 3:20 where Jesus says: "Behold, I stand at the door and knock; if any one hears My voice and opens the door, I will come into him, and will dine with him, and he with Me." But Jesus was not speaking here to *nonbelievers* outside the church about salvation. He was speaking to *Christians* within the church of Laodicea about fellowship.

In his commentary on the Book of Revelation, John Walvoord says, "This was an appeal to *Christians* rather than to non-Christians."[112] Charles Ryrie says of this verse, "Christ is appealing to the worldly, compromising *believers* in the church to return and enjoy full fellowship with Him."[113] Daniel Wallace, New Testament professor at Dallas Theological Seminary, says of Revelation 3:20, "It is not a verse about salvation at all."[114]

---

[111] Charles Spurgeon, "A Memorable Milestone," a sermon delivered on March 25, 1886.

[112] See Walvoord's comments at Revelation 3:20 in *The Bible Knowledge Commentary*. Emphasis mine.

[113] See Ryrie's notes at Revelation 3:20 in *The Ryrie Study Bible*. Emphasis mine.

[114] Daniel B. Wallace, "Revelation 3:20 and the Offer of Salvation," http://bible.org/article/revelation-320-and-offer-salvation.

One of the reasons Wallace, Walvoord, Ryrie and other Bible commentators have concluded this verse speaks about believers is because Jesus said in Revelation 3:22, "He who has an ear, let him hear what the Spirit says to the *churches.*" People within the churches who have grown spiritually weak and out of fellowship with Jesus can renew their fellowship with their willing and gracious Savior by simply responding to His request to come in and dine with them.

A second reason I think this cliché ("Ask Jesus into your heart...") needs to be shelved is because it is confusing to nonbelievers. Many of them wonder what in the world the phrase even means when they hear a well-meaning Christian say it—*Invite Jesus into my heart? How does He get in there? How does He breathe in there? How can He live in my heart and someone else's heart also?*

So, for these reasons and others, instead of using these clichés—"Give your heart (or life) to Christ and be saved" or "Invite Jesus into your heart"—why not urge your listeners to:

- "Believe in the Lord Jesus, and you will be saved" (Acts 16:31)

- "Repent, and each of you be baptized in the name of Jesus Christ for the forgiveness of your sins; and you will receive the gift of the Holy Spirit" (Acts 2:38)

- "Confess with your mouth Jesus as Lord, and believe in your heart that God raised Him from the dead, [and] you will be saved" (Rom. 10:9)

- "Repent and turn to God" (Acts 26:20)

56. Speak to persuade.

*Paul "entered the synagogue and continued
speaking out boldly for three months, reasoning
and persuading them about the kingdom
of God." (Acts 19:8)*

After taking over a new church, a pastor was highly compli-
mented on his first sermon. A number of people told him it
was just what the congregation needed. The next Sunday he
preached well again, but the congregation was greatly puzzled
because he preached the same sermon as before. The third
Sunday, when the same sermon was preached again, the people
came to the preacher for an explanation. He said, "Why, yes it
is the same sermon. You told me the first Sunday how much
you needed just that, and I watched all week for some change
in your lives, but there was none, so I preached it again. I
watched all next week; still no change; and I don't see any yet.
Don't you think I'd better prepare to preach it again next Sunday?"[115]

I don't recommend you do what that pastor did, but the
story does illustrate something important for us. One of the
goals in preaching God's Word is *persuasion*—persuading
people to not only believe what the passage says, but to act
upon it, to move, to change direction, etc.

God forbid our listeners just be hearers of the Word and
not doers (James 1:22). As preachers, we are, as J. I. Packer
puts it, "seeking unashamedly to change the way people think

---

[115] *Illustrations of Bible Truths*, compiled by Ruth Peters, QuickVerse.

and live."[116] Changing the way people think and live is ultimately the responsibility of the people hearing the teaching and the Holy Spirit. But the Spirit uses the preacher and his persuasive words in the process. Martyn Lloyd-Jones said:

> Surely the whole object of this act [of preaching] is to persuade people. The preacher does not just say things with the attitude of 'take it or leave it.' He desires to persuade them of the truth of his message; he wants them to see it; he is trying to do something to them, to influence them…he wants to move them, to take them with him, to lead them to the Truth.[117]

How should we seek to persuade people to act upon the Word, to change direction, etc.? I know of no other way from the pulpit except to lay open before the people what the Scriptures say, show the people how reasonable God's requests are, remind them how worthy God is of our trust and obedience, and then tell them what God desires they do. So, we're not just at the pulpit seeking to *educate* people about what the Bible says and what certain people did, we're going beyond that. We're trying to show them the beauty of God's Word and will for their lives. And then we exhort them:

- "Go and do the same!" (Luke 10:37)
- "God desires you to obey Him in this area"
- "You need to change direction"
- "Do this and you will live" (Luke 10:28)
- "Don't just believe what we're reading—the

---

[116] Cited by Wallace Benn, "Preaching with a Pastor's Heart: Richard Baxter's *The Reformed Pastor*," in *Preach the Word: Essays on Expository Preaching in Honor of R. Kent Hughes*, 137.

[117] Martyn Lloyd-Jones, *Preaching & Preachers*, 91–92.

demons believe—act on it!"

One of the questions that immediately comes up in some people's minds after exhortations like these, is *Why? Why does God want me to live this way?* One of the ways to be more effective in persuading people to act on what the Scriptures say is to answer this *Why?* question. This brings me to my next point.

57. Help your listeners understand *why* God requires a particular action.

> *"For this very reason, make every effort to..."* (2 Pet. 1:5)

We previously talked about answering the six big questions (Who? What? Where? Why? etc.). This "Why?" question is a little different. When you are teaching, one of the questions on the minds of your listeners is:

> Why should I do this? Yes, I understand that God desires for me to (fill in the blank), but *why*? Why does He desire I live that way?

It is important to answer that question.

If a father interrupts his kids while they're playing out in front of the house after school and says, "Come in and put some nice clothes on," his kids are naturally going to want to know *why*. Now, the father could just exert his authority as the parent and say, "Because I said to. That's why." And the kids would obey—hopefully—though there would probably be some grumbling. But if the father takes the time to explain to them, "I told you to come in and put some nice clothes on because we are leaving the house; we're going out to dinner at a nice restaurant," the children are much more likely to joyfully carry out his request.

Well, the same is true with the people we teach. They are much more likely to joyfully carry out God's instructions if they know *why* God tells them to do something, especially if they can see how reasonable God's instructions are—how rooted they are in His wise plan for humanity's wellbeing.

Sometimes the answer to the *why* question will be right there in the passage you are teaching from. Other times it won't be. Having a good understanding of the Scriptures will obviously be of great benefit in those cases. But here is a quick tip. The answers to the *why* questions are often related to:

- Who God is
- What God has done for sinners
- What He has in store in the future for those who obey or disobey

You'll see that in the following examples:

- Forgive others
  Why? God forgave us (Eph. 4:32)

- Walk in love
  Why? Christ loved us (Eph. 5:1–2)

- Be holy
  Why? God is holy (1 Pet. 1:16)

- Don't judge one another
  Why? Christ is the judge (Jn. 5:22; Rom. 14:4)

153

- Flee sexual immorality
  Why? Your body is a temple of the Holy Spirit. You are not your own, you were bought with a price (1 Cor. 6:18–20)

- Repent and trust in Christ
  Why? There is a day of judgment coming (Rom. 2:5–6)

Of course, these aren't the only answers to these *why* questions, but you can see how explaining these truths would help to motivate your listeners to obey.

58. Restate the important stuff.

"Rejoice in the Lord always; again
I will say, rejoice!" (Phil. 4:4)

One of the communication tools an inexperienced teacher often neglects to use is *restatement* or *repetition*. It shows right at the outset of his teaching. The young man will say, "Open your Bibles with me to such and such a verse," then he will pray and start reading. Well, experience tells us that as people start reaching for their Bibles, only about two-thirds of them remember what verse he asked them to turn to. When he starts reading, a third of the congregation is looking around wondering, "What verse did he say?"

The obvious way to avoid this problem is to restate the verse a few seconds after first mentioning it. If you are using PowerPoint or Keynote, you might also put the verse reference on the screen so that people can look and see it.

Restating your main points is also important (especially for note takers). If you say, "Here we see a fifth truth: Justification is by grace alone through faith in Christ alone," and then keep talking without restating your point, only about a fourth of those taking notes are going to get what you said down on paper and another fourth are going to write it down wrong ("Justification is by Christ's faith in us alone").

Years ago when I was a new believer, a pastor said, "It's important that we know *what* we believe and *why* we believe it." He didn't repeat his point, but I thought it was important enough to write down in the margin of my Bible. And so I did—in pen, unfortunately. I say unfortunately because a year or two later I realized I had totally botched what the preacher said. I wrote down, "Know what *they* believe and why we believe it." It is there in my Bible to this day. Although I've drawn a line through it and corrected the wording, it serves as a reminder of the importance of restating the important stuff.

In addition to restating verse references you ask people to turn to and your important points, it is also good to occasionally reread an entire verse, even slowing down over key words as you read it the second time. Doing this, will allow the listeners more time to really process what the Bible is saying.

59. Honor your spouse and family in the pulpit.

"Show her honor as a fellow heir of the grace of life." (1 Pet. 3:7)

Don't use your spouse's or your children's weaknesses and downfalls as material for an illustration. This should go without saying, but I hear this very thing happening. The pastor hesitates for a moment—as his conscience says, "Don't do it!"—and then he continues, "My wife is going to kill me for telling you this…but occasionally she struggles with (fill in the blank) and the other day when I came home from church…"

And there sits the pastor's wife, sinking down into the pew. And everyone who knows she's the pastor's wife is looking at her to see her reaction.

I don't think pastors should do this. We are to be role models (1 Tim. 4:12) to the men in the church in how to love (Eph. 5:25) and honor our wives as Christ loves the church. I never read of Jesus publicly displaying the sins of his followers for the sake of an illustration. Why not? Love covers a multitude of sins (1 Pet. 4:8).

If you desire for the husbands you teach to love and honor *their* wives, model that for them and honor *your* wife.

The same goes for your children. So few youth survive the transitional challenges of growing up in a church and then going from the high school ministry to attending church in the main sanctuary on their own. Don't put another obstacle in their way by telling the congregation about their struggles and weaknesses. What child of a preacher is going to want to hang out with a sanctuary full of adults who have heard about the sins of his youth? None I've met.

If you're going to cast someone in bad light for the sake of an illustration or humorous story, make sure the person goes nameless or that the leading character is you.

60. Use humor wisely.

"If by a laugh I can make men see the
folly of an error better than in any other way,
they shall laugh."[118] –Charles Spurgeon

I love to laugh and I enjoy making people laugh. You're probably the same. And a strong case can be made that Jesus made people laugh. Lines like, "Why do you look at the speck in your brother's eye, but do not notice the log that is in your own eye?" (Matt. 7:3) surely drew a laugh from His listeners—even as they were being confronted with a heart-penetrating truth.

I believe there is a place for humor as we teach. God created laughter. A joyful heart is good medicine (Prov. 17:22). But be careful that your humor is relevant, helpful, and God-honoring (1 Cor. 10:31). Here are some words of counsel:

- **Don't feel like you need to start every sermon with a joke or funny story**

For whatever reason, this has become very popular in church services in America. Perhaps pastors have been influenced by David Letterman or other late night television personalities. Letterman, Leno and others typically open their shows with a humorous monologue to much applause. When it comes to doing something like that at church to kick off a sermon, I agree with Warren Wiersbe:

> It is a mystery to us why some preachers think they must always tell a joke before they read their text and preach the message. When there is a hostile audience or an atmos-

---

[118] Charles Spurgeon, "Five Fears," a sermon delivered August 23, 1857.

phere of tension, perhaps a bit of humor can help to change that atmosphere; but certainly this is an exception. Can you imagine Peter telling a joke before he preached at Pentecost, or Paul entertaining the philosophers on Mars Hill?[119]

It's pretty hard to imagine Peter or Paul doing that. And that should cause all of us who teach God's Word to prayerfully consider whether *we* should do it, and if so, how often. Emil Turner points out that:

> Humor is not necessary to put a congregation at ease. We use it to put *ourselves* at ease. But your call, your preparation, the sense of God's presence, your prayer life—these things give you a true sense of "ease" in preaching.[120]

Well said. The congregation is usually already at ease. They've seen and chatted with friends. They've spent time worshipping the Lord. If you are using humor at the beginning of a message to put yourself at ease, consider again Turner's words above. Putting *oneself* at ease is not a good reason for an ambassador of the King to begin a message with something funny.

- **Be careful to avoid humor that insults or ridicules**

I used to start off a teaching on evidence for God's existence with a joke that someone emailed me years ago. It went like this:

---

[119] Warren Wiersbe and David Wiersbe, *The Elements of Preaching*, 76.

[120] Emil Turner, "The Use of Humor in the Pulpit," emphasis mine. http://www.absc.org/emil-turner-executive-director-of-the-arkansas-baptist-state-convention/111-default-category/915-the-use-of-humor-in-the-pulpit.html.

An elementary school teacher explained to her class of young children that she was an atheist. She asked her class if they were atheists too. Not really knowing what atheism was but wanting to be like their teacher, their hands went flying into the air. There was, however, one exception. A girl named Lucy had not gone along with the crowd. The teacher asked her why she decided to be different. Lucy said, "Because I'm not an atheist." The teacher then asked, "What are you?" Lucy said, "I'm a Christian." She asked Lucy why she was a Christian. "Well, I was brought up knowing and loving Jesus. My mom is a Christian, and my dad is a Christian, so I am a Christian." The teacher angrily said, "That's no reason! What if your mom was a moron, and your dad was a moron? What would you be then?" Lucy paused, thought about it and said, "Then, I'd be an atheist."[121]

Lucy's response always received a thunderous laugh. But, it finally dawned on me that, as funny as the joke is, Lucy's response falls short of God's standard in 1 Peter 3:8–9:

> To sum up, all of you be harmonious, sympathetic, brotherly, kindhearted, and humble in spirit; *not returning evil for evil* or *insult for insult*, but giving a blessing instead; for you were called for the very purpose that you might inherit a blessing.

In the joke, the teacher insults Lucy ("That's no response!"). A proper God-honoring response by Lucy would not include an insult about being an atheistic "moron."

---

[121] Original source unknown.

So, although the story drew a large amount of laughter and segued nicely into the topic at hand, I decided to pull the plug on it.

- **Realize humor can erect obstacles to a person receiving the Word**

Looking back now, I'm sure the joke about Lucy probably bothered atheists who may have been in our midst. To think now that an atheist may have come to church for the first time to see what Christians were all about or to give the Bible a chance, *only to hear me telling a joke about atheists*, makes me cringe with regret!

Jokes often come at the expense of an individual or particular group of people (short people, older folks, women, computer "geeks," etc.). You might think your joke is "innocent" and that people "understand your heart" and know that you "really don't mean it," etc. And many will agree with you along those lines. But the laughs you get from jokes that call attention to a certain type of people will often cause the people from that group in your congregation to have a challenging time listening to you after that. Is that what you want? Do you want to erect obstacles to the Word of God doing its work? Paul said, "We put no obstacle in anyone's way, so that no fault may be found with our ministry" (2 Cor. 6:3 ESV).

- **Put yourself in their shoes before you tell the joke**

When considering whether or not to say something humorous, try to place yourself in the shoes of the person or group who might be offended. With the atheist joke I told, I should have asked myself, "Self, if you were visiting a lecture by an atheist on evidence for atheism—if there was evidence for atheism—

and he started off with a joke about how moronic Christians are, how would you feel?" Ouch. Well, that settles it. Ditch that joke. Jesus said, "In *everything*, therefore, treat people the same way you want them to treat you" (Matt. 7:12).

- **Avoid getting laughs at a family member's expense**

A long time after your congregation has forgotten your sermon, your family members will remember being the source of laughter.[122] Your wife might be strong enough to handle the lampooning, but your kids aren't. Don't sacrifice them on comedy's altar for the sake of a laugh. If you do this on an ongoing basis, you can count on your kids leaving your church when they are old enough to go somewhere else.

- **The best humor is self deprecating**

People enjoy hearing a teacher tell of an embarrassing moment or of being caught in uncomfortable circumstances.[123]

May the Lord give you wisdom when it comes to being humorous at the pulpit.

61. Be careful about teaching too long.

> *"And as Paul kept on talking, he [Eutychus] was overcome by sleep and fell down from the third floor and was picked up dead." (Acts 20:9)*

---

[122] Emil Turner, "The Use of Humor in the Pulpit."
[123] Ibid.

How long you teach depends on the audience, the setting, the topic, the temperature, your ability to keep the congregation interested, etc. So, I won't say here how long you should preach. I trust that God will give you wisdom regarding that. But, I would like to give some advice here to those of you who will be invited to teach in places away from your preaching home.

If you are asked to be a guest teacher somewhere, make sure you ask ahead of time how long they would like you to teach. You do not want to assume you are going to have forty-five to sixty minutes and then find out shortly before you teach that you only have thirty. I've been in that situation and it can be stressful trying to figure out what to cut from the message right before you're suppose to teach.

If the worship team or announcements go long—and for some reason they usually do when there is a guest speaker—then allow the Holy Spirit to help you edit your message on the spot as you speak. Do not say to yourself, "Well, they told me I could teach forty-five minutes and that I should wrap it up by 9:45, but they went long, so I'm going to still teach for forty-five minutes and I'll just end at 9:55." Don't do that. End on time. There is usually a good reason someone told you to end by a particular time. The church probably needs to allow enough time between worship gatherings for the parking lot to empty so that people arriving for the next service can find a spot to park.

If there are multiple morning services at the venue you're asked to teach at, I suggest writing the end of each service time on a piece of paper and placing it on the pulpit so that you can keep an eye on the clock and make sure you finish on time.

THE PREACHER'S BODY LANGUAGE

62. When teaching, try to maintain consistent eye contact with your listeners.

"Looking at them, Jesus said..."
(Mk. 10:27)

Maintaining eye contact with people while you teach is of course very important. Many people have a hard time listening attentively to a teacher who does not regularly take his eyes off his notes to look at them. Here are some practical suggestions to help you get your eyes off of your notes:

A. Keep the paragraphs in your notes short.

Many inexperienced teachers bring pages of notes to the pulpit that no experienced teacher would attempt to teach from. Their paragraphs have 20 lines of text; none of the words are highlighted or in bold fonts. No wonder they have to look down at their notes so often! They looked up for a brief second and now they are trying to figure out where they were.

I encourage you to keep your paragraphs short (three to five sentences is probably a good guideline). Let your notes breathe. Put space between your paragraphs. Don't try to fit everything on two or three pages of notes.

B. Highlight a key word or two in each paragraph.

Use a neon marker to highlight key words or phrases in each paragraph. This will allow you to look down with just a glance, see the key word, and recall the key thought of the paragraph.

C. Print out your notes early.

One of the best ways to get your eyes off your notes is to print out your notes early enough to go over them three or four times. Going over your notes more than once will help embed what you want to say in your memory. If you print out your notes half an hour before you teach and quickly skim through them, you're probably going to be reading your notes at the pulpit.

D. Draw on your notes.

There's a reason why the Macintosh computer I'm typing on right now has little icons down across the bottom of the screen.

Those small pictures are there to remind me what is going to happen if I click on them. I look down at the small picture of a fox wrapped around a globe and I remember that is my Firefox web browser. If I click on that, I'm going to access the Internet. Icons and pictures can very quickly remind us of a great deal.

Realizing that was the case, years ago I started drawing little icons, symbols, and stick figures in the margins of my notes. When I glance down at my notes and see a cloud, tree or stick figure on his knees, I can more easily recall what I want to say.

Although this is an unorthodox suggestion here—I have never seen this recommended in any of the books on preaching I've read—I encourage you to try this. I have found it to be quite helpful.

E. Read ahead while people are turning in their Bibles.

In the middle of your message when you say, "Turn with me in your Bibles to John, chapter twenty," start reviewing your notes. Look ahead to see what you plan on saying after the reading. Page turning offers you a good ten to fifteen-second window to look down at your notes. Of course this will only work if you don't need to spend long turning there yourself. You can accomplish this with a bookmark or two or by embedding the relevant Scriptures right into your notes.

F. Use a wireless microphone.

A podium microphone generally requires that you stand close to the podium, which in turn requires you to tilt your head down about forty-five degrees to see your notes. Each time you do that the congregation gets a shot of the top of your head. Wearing a wireless lapel or over-the-ear microphone will allow you to back away from the podium a couple of feet. This way, you do not have to tilt your head down as much to see your notes. This will make it less obvious you are looking down at your notes.

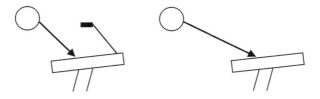

Line of sight with **podium** mic   Line of sight with **wireless** mic

Here is another bit of advice worth mentioning when it comes to maintaining good eye contact. Try to avoid focusing too long on a particular group of people in the sanctuary. That can be distracting for people. The people you neglect to look at wonder:

- Why does he rarely look over at us?
- Is there someone over on our side he doesn't like?
- Is he talking to us or is he just talking to them?

So, look at people all around the room. Talk with one listener at a time for a second or two and move from person to person. Not only will they benefit, but you will also. Doing this will help you discern how well the people are tracking with you. If you say something and see people tilting their heads, dropping their jaws and staring back at you with confused looks on their faces, well, that's a good indicator you need to elaborate a little or possibly share an illustration to clarify what you said. If you see people nodding off, you might share a story to draw them back in.

63. Avoid distracting body language in the pulpit.

"Sir, we wish to see Jesus."
(Jn. 12:21)

When God's people come to a worship gathering, they are not coming to see us. They are there to worship the Lord and hear from His Word. Knowing this, the wise preacher will try to become as transparent as possible by minimizing distracting behavior at the pulpit. Here are some of the more common distractions:

A. Looking like a statue

Minimizing distractions doesn't mean you stand motionless. Haddon Robinson reminds us that, "God designed the human body to move. If your congregation wants to look at a statue, they can go to a museum...You need to carry over into preaching the same freedom you give to your hands, arms, and head in personal conversation."[124]

B. Pacing back and forth

If you are speaking into a microphone attached to the podium you will have to stay put. If you use a wireless microphone, remember that pacing is often associated with worry or nervousness.

C. Scratching your head

---

[124] Haddon Robinson, *Biblical Preaching*, 207–208.

D. Twisting a ring

E. Looking at your watch

F. Holding the pulpit tightly and never letting go

G. Picking food out of your teeth

H. Picking your nose

I've seen it all—yes, even this last one. Yes, at the pulpit. Your family and friends may not consider these sorts of things very distracting, but obviously all of these could be a distraction in a public setting.

I encourage you to watch some video footage of yourself teaching. This can be a humbling experience but well worth the humiliation! Watching yourself flapping your arms all over the place or scratching your head as you say *"Umm," "You know,"* or *"I was like"* more times than you can count, can lead to immediate improvements.

THE PREACHER AFTER THE SERMON

64. Don't judge yourself by men's praise or lack of it.

"Those who disagree with us vent their grumblings on their wives and friends, out of our hearing."[125] –F. B. Meyer

Hearing some positive feedback after a well-taught study can be a great encouragement. But if you seek to judge your teaching abilities by the praise (encouraging feedback) of men, you

---

[125] F. B. Meyer, *Jottings and Hints for Lay Preachers*, 120.

are in for an emotional roller coaster ride. The praises of men are not always a reliable measuring rod.

The ones who come and seek to encourage you are often people who love you. It is rare that those who thought...

- Your introduction was confusing
- Your delivery was challenging to sit through
- Your story to illustrate a point seemed disconnected
- Your joke offended them
- Your conclusion was weak

...will come and tell you. Very rarely do the ones who disagree with you or spot an error or mistake in your interpretation of a passage, come up and say anything. And even when they do, they'll often still tell you, "Good job today!" because they don't want to discourage you.

If we could hear some of the comments and complaints about our preaching in the car rides home, as husbands and wives vent their frustration, we would be brought to our knees and greatly humbled.

So, be careful. Don't bask in the compliments you receive and think you have arrived as a preacher. If you look at yourself through the eyes of those who love you and compliment you on your fine job of teaching, you'll be tempted to be prideful and content with where you are as a preacher. And if you think you *are* a great teacher, that could thwart any desire to improve.

You also need to be careful to not read too much into those times when a criticism comes your way or no one has an encouraging word for you after you teach. If you mull those situations over too long you will be more prone to abandon your post prematurely or waste valuable time sulking in depression. I know this from experience.

When I started teaching a weekly Bible Study to a small gathering of surfers and their girlfriends in Point Loma, California, in 1994, I was encouraged by the gracious words of those who talked to me afterwards. And I needed the encouragement. Truthfully, I thought the studies were pretty weak. But soon, without realizing it, I became somewhat *dependent* upon encouraging feedback. I realized this when I joined the pastoral staff at Calvary Chapel Vista in 1997. There were numerous times, early on, when I would teach the college group and not hear a word of encouragement from anyone when I was done. I soon began to think, *"I must really be a horrible teacher! The people are obviously not blessed; they are not saying anything!"* There were times when I nearly quit because I was overwhelmed with discouragement!

I finally realized that a preacher must not look for the applause of men to validate his ministry. We must seek the applause of Heaven. The only approval that really matters is God's. Paul told Timothy, "Be diligent to present yourself approved to [Who?] *God"* (2 Tim. 2:15). That's what matters—God's approval. So, I encourage you to ask yourself after your time of teaching:

- What would the *Lord* think of my preaching?
- Was it pleasing to *Him*?
- Am I acceptable *to Him* as a preacher of His Word?

Seek to have God's approval of your teaching and you'll need no one else's.

65. Find someone who will offer suggestions and constructive criticism.

"But when Priscilla and Aquila heard him,
they took him aside and explained to him the way
of God more accurately." (Acts 18:26)

Dr. Clarence Bass, professor emeritus at Bethel Theological Seminary, early in his ministry, preached in a church in Los Angeles. He thought he had done quite well as he stood at the door greeting people as they left the sanctuary. The remarks about his preaching were complimentary. That is, until a little old man commented, "You preached too long."

The professor wasn't fazed by the remark, especially in light of the many positive comments. "You didn't preach loud enough," came another negative comment; it was from the same little old man.

Dr. Bass thought it strange that the man had come through the line twice, but when the same man came through the line a third time and exclaimed, "You used too many big words"— this called for some explanation.

Dr. Bass sought out a deacon who stood nearby and asked him, "Do you see that little old man over there? Who is he?"

"Don't pay any attention to him," the deacon replied. "All he does is go around and repeat everything he hears."[126]

As painful as feedback like that can be to hear, we all can benefit having a Priscilla, Aquila (Acts 18:26) or Paul (Gal. 2:11) who can offer wise, loving, constructive feedback regarding

---

[126] *Pulpit and Bible Study Helps*, Vol. 16, #5, 1. http://bible.org/illustration/he-repeats-everything-he-hears.

our teachings. The feedback they provide can be discouraging at times for the faint at heart but very helpful for the teacher who realizes there is room to improve.

You may not have to ask anyone to help you with this, as the story above illustrates. Plenty of people over the years have lovingly offered unsolicited feedback to me:

- "You need to slow down"
- "Too much information for us to take notes"
- "The circumference of the Earth you stated was actually the diameter"
- "The verse reference you cited was wrong"
- "That joke offended my friend"
- "Irenaeus is not pronounced like that"

They may come to you as well. And praise the Lord for them! If no one is giving you constructive criticism, I encourage you to ask a person or two (who are mature in the Lord and who you think have good opinions about what good preaching is) to keep their eyes and ears open while you teach for ways you might improve.

Ask if they would prayerfully consider giving you constructive and even critical feedback. You might say to them, "I trust that with God's help I can improve as a teacher. I certainly feel like there's room for growth. I would love to get some constructive feedback and criticism when you think it would help me improve. Would you pray about helping me out in this way?"

This obviously takes some courage and humility to ask someone to do this. If the person says "Yes," be prepared to graciously receive some criticism and probably humorous feedback.

A couple of days ago I was teaching at a church that I have taught at many times. After the teaching, an older couple came over to me and the woman said, "I like how you're including some humor in your messages now. That's new! I like that."

What seemed like a compliment—and it was on one hand—actually felt like a humorous criticism. Why? I feel like I've *always* included some humor in my messages. According to her though, this was something brand new!

Then right on the heels of her feedback, her husband said, "And you are speaking slower now. You used to go so fast and give us so much information; it was hard to keep up with you. I appreciate the new slower pace."

I didn't know what to say. I almost laughed out loud at the content of these compliments! As was the case with my use of humor, I didn't think my pacing was any different that day than the way I had been teaching for years. Either way, God bless this couple. Their compliments, with small criticisms tucked inside, were a blessing to receive. May the Lord bring brothers and sisters like them into your life—people who are willing to share the truth in love regarding your preaching. Every teacher can benefit from them.

66. Remember your preaching continues after you've stepped down from the pulpit.

"Out of one hundred men, one will read the Bible, the ninety-nine will read the Christian."[127]
–D. L. Moody

---

[127] Cited in Philip Yancey, *What's So Amazing About Grace?* 262.

I visited a church for a Christmas Eve service many years ago and on the way there I saw a car in my rear view mirror weaving in and out of traffic. I thought, "Whoever is driving that car is going to kill someone!" A few seconds later the driver was right behind me tailgating me. So, I slammed on my brakes. No. I kept driving and he quickly swerved around me. As he was passing me on my left, I looked over and it was the pastor of the church I was on my way to visit!

I can't remember a word that pastor said that night, but I will never forget the way he drove. Now, obviously he was running late to church. And I have driven like a mad man at times also—as I suspect you have. So, we won't hold this man's driving that night against him; I'm just pointing out that what a person *does* sticks with people much longer than what a person *says*.

The studies you teach from the pulpit will soon be forgotten—yes, even if you alliterate your main points—but what you preach by the way you live, will remain with people for a lifetime.

My friend, live out the Scriptures in a God-honoring way outside of church. Live out what you teach. Peter said, "Shepherd the flock of God…being *examples* to the flock" (1 Pet. 5:2–3). God's people need to see what following Jesus looks like in real life. Knowing this, Paul told Timothy and us by implication: "In speech, conduct, love, faith and purity, show yourself an example" (1 Tim. 4:12). Your life can and should be a great model for others to follow.

67. Be patient as God's Word germinates.

"God will hide from you much of the fruit He causes in your ministry. You will see enough to be assured of His blessing, but not so much as to think you could live without it. For God aims to exalt Himself, not the preacher."[128] *–John Piper*

Many a young teacher has wondered why there doesn't seem to be much change in the lives of those he preaches to week in and week out. The people continue to struggle with the same sins, problems and worries. They continue to seem spiritually lethargic when it's time to worship or serve—even after his carefully chosen topical messages exhorting them in those very areas.

You will probably experience this with some of your listeners as well. What's a teacher to do? Be patient with the people as God's Word does its work. Paul said, "Preach the word…with great *patience* and instruction" (2 Tim. 4:2).

Jesus likened the Word of God to seed that brings forth fruit (Mk. 4:14). Well, if you've ever planted seeds, you know that they take time to germinate, grow to maturity, and produce fruit.

So, as you sow the Word, be patient. Fruit *will* come (Isa. 55:10–11). Your labor is not in vain (1 Cor. 15:58; Gal. 6:9). God's Word will perform its work in those who believe (1 Thes. 2:13). Knowing this, Charles Spurgeon said:

---

[128] John Piper, *The Supremacy of God in Preaching*, 19.

Take it as a rule that the truth of God prayed over, spoken in the fear of the Lord, with the Holy Spirit dwelling in the man who speaks it, will produce the effect which is natural to it…We know that our labor is not in vain in the Lord. I do not come into this pulpit myself with any fear that I shall preach in vain. It does not occur to me that such a thing can happen.[129]

68. Spend time with other teachers.

"I went up to Jerusalem to become acquainted with Cephas." (Gal. 1:18)

If you don't have good friendships with others who preach the Word, pray that God would provide that for you. What a blessing it is to have friends who can:

- Offer advice
- Pray for you
- Encourage you
- Recommend good commentaries and books
- Give you good ideas on a variety of matters—how they've handled criticism, dealt with a difficult passage of Scripture, etc.

And I encourage you to be on the look out for other teachers *you* can encourage as well.

---

[129] Charles Spurgeon, "The Cause and Cure of Weariness in Sunday School Teachers" an address delivered on November 8, 1877.

69. Expose yourself to great preaching.

"I pity the preacher who only listens to one preacher, especially if he is that one preacher!"[130]*–H. B. Charles*

One of the best ways to learn how to preach well is to listen to or read sermons by great preachers. Here are some teachers you might consider, in alphabetical order by last name:[131]

Donald Grey Barnhouse
Alistair Begg
James Montgomery Boice
Brian Brodersen
R. Kent Hughes
Harry Ironside
Martyn Lloyd-Jones
John MacArthur
J. Vernon McGee

F. B. Meyer
G. Campbell Morgan
Alan Redpath
Oswald Sanders
Chuck Smith
Charles Spurgeon
Ray Stedman
A. W. Tozer
Warren Wiersbe

Many of the sermons by the men above are available to read or listen to online. Not only will you be edified listening to their teachings, you will learn some important lessons about preaching.

---

[130] H. B. Charles, Jr., "How Did You Develop Your Style of Preaching?" http://www.hbcharlesjr.com/2012/07/24/how-did-you-develop-your-style-of-preaching.

[131] The inclusion of a man on this list does not mean I endorse every aspect of his theology. I do have small disagreements with some of them on certain matters, but nevertheless, they are still considered by many today to be great preachers.

70. Try to avoid picking up the mannerisms and sayings of popular teachers. Be yourself.

"The worst preachers are those who mimic others."[132]*–Charles Spurgeon*

It is very easy, especially early on in your calling to teach, to consider yourself and think, *"Let's be honest. I'm not very good at this. So and so is good at this. I think I'll just try to sound more like him. I love the way he teaches."*

Many teachers who have had their eyes too much upon themselves and their own shortcomings (I'm including myself here!) have fallen into the trap of trying to imitate someone God has blessed as a teacher.

But God created that man to be that man. And He created you to be you! If He wanted two Johnny Nonotes, Bob Funnymans, Stephen Greekgurus or David Radiovoices, *He would have made two of them.* But He didn't. There's only one of each of them. And you are the only you. God created you uniquely. And He placed you in the body of Christ just as He pleased. So, seek to be *that* person, the tool God created *you* to be. A Holy Spirit-filled you.

Now, having said this, I do want to point out that there is a difference between imitating someone's unique style, personality, mannerisms, voice, etc. and imitating someone's godly character or faith. If you appreciate someone's high view of Scripture, their commitment to addressing difficult passages of Scripture, their love for people, etc., then of course, by all means, learn from them, follow in their footsteps and even

---

[132] Charles Spurgeon, "Christ Lifted Up," a sermon delivered on July 5, 1857.

imitate them. The writer of the Book of Hebrews said, "Remember those who led you, who spoke the word of God to you; and considering the result of their conduct, *imitate their faith*" (Heb. 13:7). Paul wrote, "Brethren, join in *following my example*, and observe those who walk according to the pattern you have in us" (Phil. 3:17). So there is a place for imitation.

The imitation I'm advocating against is the imitation of peculiar sayings, movements, talking style, voice inflections, etc. Imitation of this sort can be spotted a mile away. The danger in engaging in this kind of imitation (deliberately or not) is that it will hinder some people's ability to receive truth from you. Some will think, "This guy is trying to sound like (your favorite teacher). What a fake! He's not being real with us. I wonder what else is fake about this guy?!"

Obviously, we don't want that to happen. So, be yourself. Rest in who God created you to be. Be the Holy Spirit-filled you!

71. Remember that success in preaching is pleasing God not reaching large numbers.

"Do right: when you have done so, the rest lies with God."[133]–C. S. Lewis

A young man had just become pastor of a large church. At a reception given him by his people, one of the gossips, a woman with a dangerous tongue, came up and said, "I do not understand how you dared attempt the task of pleasing seven hundred people." Quick as a flash he replied, "I did not come to this city to please seven hundred people. I have to please only One; and

---

[133] C. S. Lewis, *The Collected Letters of C. S. Lewis*, Vol. 2, 174.

if I please Him, all will be well."[134] Pleasing God and trusting Him with the results—words of wisdom there.

Many teachers of God's Word grow discouraged if their churches or Bible study groups don't steadily grow into what they think are healthy size gatherings. It can be easy to think, "I must not be called to teach. I've been teaching for five years and there are only 75 people attending our gatherings."

This is a conclusion that many pastors have drawn. But the size of a congregation is not a reliable indicator as to whether or not a person is called by God to teach or not.

- Some of the "word of faith" teachers, who espouse all kinds of heresy, have enormous churches
- The Mormon church is growing by leaps and bounds
- Jeremiah preached 40 years with apparently only two converts: Baruch, his scribe (Jer. 32:12, 36:1–4, 45:1–5) and Ebed-melech, an Ethiopian eunuch who served the king (38:7–13, 39:15–18)
- Noah preached (2 Pet. 2:5) for perhaps 120 years (Gen. 6:3) and only a few ended up coming into the ark with him

Success is not about reaching large numbers. Success in preaching is about faithfulness. Success is about pleasing the Lord. Paul said, "we speak, not as pleasing men, but *God* who tests our hearts" (1 Thes. 2:4 NKJV). Elsewhere, he wrote, "we have as our ambition, whether at home or absent, *to be pleasing to Him*. For we must all appear before the judgment seat of Christ" (2 Cor. 5:9–10). That should be your ambition in ministry: "to be pleasing to *Him*."

---

[134] *Illustrations of Bible Truths*, compiled by Ruth Peters, QuickVerse.

Do that and then leave the breadth of your impact (the numbers you reach) up to Him. Jesus said, "*I* will build My church" (Matt. 16:18). The growth of the church is His responsibility. You be pleasing to Him.

72. Realize you'll probably never feel like you have arrived as a teacher and if you do, it's probably time to step down.

"My power is made perfect in weakness."
(2 Cor. 12:9 ESV)

G. Campbell Morgan once said that as he made his way to the pulpit each Sunday, Isaiah 53:7 repeatedly came to mind: "He was led as a lamb to the slaughter"![135] Teaching the Word of God to others is a humbling experience. I have found myself on numerous occasions, before I step up to teach, crying out to the Lord the same question the apostle Paul asked, "Who is sufficient for these things?" (2 Cor. 2:16 NKJV).

Let me assure you, if you feel *insufficient* to teach God's Word—even after ten years of teaching on a consistent basis—don't panic! You'll probably feel that way twenty years from now.

Many men who have been preaching twenty or more years still stare down at their notes before they step up to the pulpit and say, *"God, this is so weak!"* And when they're done teaching, their assessment of the study doesn't always improve. Charles Spurgeon said, "It is a long time since I preached a sermon that I was satisfied with. I scarcely recollect ever having

---

[135] Stephen Olford and David Olford, *Anointed Expository Preaching*, 239.

done so."[136] It's not uncommon for veteran preachers to walk away from the pulpit feeling as though:

- The Word could have been taught better
- The Lord deserved better
- God's people need better

Feeling that way does not mean God has not called you to teach. I agree with Spurgeon who said, "A sermon wept over is more acceptable with God than one gloried over."[137] He continues elsewhere:

> Every true minister will feel that he is deficient. He will compare himself with such men as [George] Whitfield, with such preachers as those of puritanical times, and he will say, What am I? Like a dwarf beside a giant, an ant-hill by the side of the mountain. When he retires to rest on Sabbath-night, he will toss from side to side on his bed, because he feels that he has missed the mark, that he has not had that earnestness, that solemnity, that death-like intenseness of purpose which became his position. He will accuse himself of not having dwelt enough on this point, or for having shunned the other, or not having been explicit enough on some certain subject, or expanded another too much. He will see his own faults, for God always chastises his own.[138]

---

[136] Charles Spurgeon, "Good Earnests of Great Success" a sermon delivered on January 12, 1868.

[137] Charles Spurgeon, "A Plain Man's Sermon" a sermon delivered on January 17, 1886.

[138] Charles Spurgeon, "Preach the Gospel," a sermon delivered on August 5, 1855.

That sense of deficiency, as you consider yourself and your preaching, is something the Lord will use to keep you humble and dependent on Him. If God were to grace you with the confidence and supreme teaching skills you desire, they would probably become a curse, for you would undoubtedly be filled with pride! And, as you know, "Pride goes before *destruction*, and a haughty spirit before stumbling" (Prov. 16:18).

73. Protect your relationship with the Lord.

"Watch over your heart with all diligence,
for from it flow the springs of life."
(Prov. 4:23)

One of the best things you can do for your teaching ministry is to look after your own relationship with the Lord. Jesus said, "For the mouth speaks out of that which fills the heart" (Matt. 12:34). If your heart is on fire for the Lord, it is going to show in your preaching.

Unfortunately, many pastors and teachers who start out with a fervent love for the Lord allow the cares of ministry and the world to slowly choke out that love. All the while they continue in the busyness of ministry. Friend, you must not let this happen!

But perhaps this describes where you *already* are. You've become a sermon-making machine, but there is only a flicker of love for Jesus in your heart. You are toiling and persevering in ministry but you have allowed your first love to grow cold. You have fallen into the same trap the people in Ephesus did. Jesus said to the church there, "I know your *deeds* and your *toil* and *perseverance*…But I have this against you, that you have left your first love" (Rev. 2:2, 4). They were busy about ministry, but Jesus was no longer their supreme love. There was ministry *in the name* of God without a vibrant love *for* God.

Has this happened in your life? If so, I want to encourage you to slow down or even take a break. Perhaps you need a month or longer sabbatical to draw near to the Lord, fast, pray, read your Bible—not for an upcoming sermon—but devotionally, to allow God to encourage you and revive you. And He will.[139]

> For thus says the high and exalted One Who lives forever, whose name is Holy, "I dwell on a high and holy place, and also with the contrite and lowly of spirit in order to *revive* the spirit of the lowly and to revive the heart of the contrite" (Isa. 57:15).

"But who is going to feed the flock?" you ask. You might invite some guest teachers to fill in for you. If you are a senior pastor, you might have your assistant pastors fill in for you. Whatever you do, make personal revival a number one priority.

Now, perhaps this doesn't describe where you're at. Your love for the Lord is running over. Your quiet time is rich. You delight to worship Him. Your heart is on fire for the Lord. To you, I echo Paul's exhortations:

> Be on guard for yourselves...Pay close attention to yourself and to your teaching; persevere in these things, for as you do this you will ensure salvation both for yourself and for those who hear you (Acts 20:28; 1 Tim. 4:16).

---

[139] Kent Hughes, the well-known pastor and Bible commentator, allowed all of the pastors at his church a six-month sabbatical for every seven years of service (*Preach the Word: Essays on Expository Preaching in Honor of R. Kent Hughes*, 277). I think there is some real wisdom in that.

Be on guard for yourself! Protect your relationship with the Lord. Guard your quiet time with Him.

In harmony with Paul's words above, Richard Baxter gave this exhortation to preachers in his day:

> Brethren, watch over your own heart. Keep out sinful passions and worldly inclinations. Keep up the life of faith and love. Be much at home with God. Let it be your daily, serious business to study your own heart, to subdue corruptions, and to live dependent on God. If not, then all your work that you constantly attend to will go amiss, and you will starve your hearers.[140]

Many men have not heeded this wise Biblical counsel and sadly, their lives and ministries have dried up or worse—their faith has been shipwrecked.

---

[140] Cited by Wallace Benn in *Preach the Word: Essays on Expository Preaching in Honor of R. Kent Hughes*, 132.

THE PREACHER'S STUDY TOOLS AND TECHNOLOGY

74. As finances permit, invest in a good library.

"I enjoy my library. Each book is a friend that converses with and teaches me."[141]
–Warren Wiersbe

Paul wrote to Timothy and said, "Bring the cloak that I left with Carpus at Troas when you come—and the *books*, especially the parchments" (2 Tim. 4:13 NKJV). Books were important to

---

[141] Warren Wiersbe, *A Basic Library for Bible Students*, 8.

Paul and they should be to the serious student of the Bible as well.

God has gifted certain people in the church to teach others (Eph. 4:11–13). And thankfully they have not only taught their local congregations or students at seminary, they have penned down their thoughts and comments on the Bible in book form for our benefit.

Owning good books, commentaries on the Bible, Bible encyclopedias, books on systematic theology, prophecy, Bible difficulties, etc. will allow you to check with the experts at any time and receive instruction, confirmation, and correction on a host of topics or passages of Scripture. Many of these resources come bundled together at discounted prices in Bible study software, which brings me to my next exhortation.

75. Take advantage of Bible study software.

"What used to take me months in page-flipping can now be done with the click of a mouse."[142]
–David Jeremiah

There are fabulous Bible study programs available for your computer, tablet or phone, that are brimming with good commentaries, concordances, dictionaries, encyclopedias, Hebrew and Greek lexicons, maps, photos, illustrations, etc. These programs can save you enormous amounts of time when you are preparing for a teaching. With a few clicks you can locate a verse and pull up two or three commentaries to see what they say about that particular verse.

---

[142] Logos.com/endorsements.

I have tried a few of the different programs out there. I prefer to use PC Study Bible[143] (now available for Macs as well as PCs). Other programs worth checking out are:

- Logos[144]
- Olive Tree's Bible Study App[145]
- Accordance[146]

If you are unable to afford software, there are some great websites that provide a plethora of *free* Bible study aids. Check out: Biblos.com, BibleStudytools.com, BlueLetterBible.org, EnduringWord.com.

76. Record your teachings.

*"This will be written for the generation
to come, that a people yet to be created may
praise the LORD." (Ps. 102:18)*

Aren't you glad God had the Bible written down for us? Putting the words of Scripture down on paper (papyrus, leather, etc.) helped ensure the permanency and accuracy of the words so that future generations, like ours, could know and walk in the truth. I suggest that you do the same thing.

In addition to preserving your teaching notes on paper or on your computer, I also encourage you to record the audio of your teachings. Recording the audio of your messages, even

---

[143] BibleSoft.com

[144] Logos.com

[145] OliveTree.com

[146] AccordanceBible.com

if you think your mom may be the only one who will listen to them, is good to do for at least three reasons:

A. The recording will serve as a future study aid.
You will probably forget your study six months from now. But you may have the opportunity to teach it again somewhere else down the road. If you have a recording of it, you can go back over it and refresh your memory. You might say, "But Charlie, I have my notes. I can go over them." I encourage you to do that, but there are things you will say when you teach that are *not* in your notes and I personally think some of those things are good to capture and prayerfully consider adding to future editions of the same study.

B. Listening to yourself teach will help you discover ways to improve your delivery.

Among other things, listening to yourself teach a few times with a critical ear will help you realize how many unnecessary *umms*, *ands*, *uhs*, *sos*, *likes* and *aaahs*, you use. Recognizing those exist is the first step to cutting them out. If you have never listened to yourself teach, I will warn you that it can be pretty discouraging, but it is a great way to discover where you can improve. So, listen to yourself, weep and cry, and then ask God to help you improve.

C. Your teaching can reach beyond your original listeners.

People may ask for a copy of the teaching for friends, family, coworkers, etc. if they know that the message was recorded. A recording allows God's Word to reach beyond the initial setting in which it was first delivered.

77. If you use PowerPoint or Keynote, use it wisely.

"Look at the birds of the air...Observe how the lilies of the field grow." (Matt. 6:26, 28)

I realized many years ago when I was teaching, that showing people large, high-resolution color photographs of:

- the Sea of Galilee
- a map of Israel
- ruins of the theater in Ephesus
- an archaeological discovery
- the interior of a cell

...would make a much longer impression on them than just talking about those things. I started doing that and immediately began receiving positive feedback from people.

It appears that Jesus and other New Testament teachers knew the value of visual aids as well. Jesus often said things like, "Look at the fig tree" or "Observe how the lilies of the field grow" (Lk. 21:29 ESV; Matt. 6:28). James said, "Look at the ships" (James 3:4). Visual aids can help make a lesson easier to understand and more memorable. As it has often been said, "A picture is worth a thousand words."

Knowing this, many preachers today are taking advantage of PowerPoint or Keynote presentation software when teaching. I don't recommend that every teacher do this. Searching for photographs and building a slide presentation can take up valuable time that might be better spent studying, preparing the sermon, praying or visiting people in your congregation.

If you do decide to use visuals, here are some important guidelines:

A. Make sure people can read your slides.

A very common mistake people make using PowerPoint is putting too many words on a single slide. Not only do their slides end up looking too busy, the people in the back half of the room can't read the small font. So, use a large enough font so all can read. Break up long quotes into two or three slides rather than squeezing the whole quote on to one slide.

B. Let the text on the slide breathe.

Don't put words right up against the edge of the screen. I see this a lot. It doesn't look good. There's a reason why every publisher in the world leaves a blank margin around the text in the  books they publish. Follow their lead and give a nice even margin of breathing space around your words (See figure above. Keep text in the gray zone). If you don't do this, your slides will look too busy.

C. Don't get so creative that the slide becomes distracting.

Don't put a Scripture or an important point on a slide that has moving things swirling about (e.g., waves rolling up on the seashore, planets spinning through the heavens). People will watch the moving part of the slide rather than read the text.

Then, they'll start wondering, "What beach is that?" or "What planet is that?" rather than pondering what the text has to say.

D. Put words on top of a plain background.

Placing your text over a photograph of trees, clouds, buildings, etc., makes the text hard to read. Check out your favorite magazine. You'll notice that good graphic artists always try to put the text over a part of the photograph that is very plain (e.g., a glassy lake or clear sky). If your photograph doesn't have a plain area to do this, crop the photo and put your text against the plain background of the slide.

E. Don't use colors that clash.

I've seen some presentations where the speaker used yellow and red fonts—on the *same* slide. I'm no Martha Stewart, but I don't think these are good colors to use, especially on the same slide. What book or magazine have you read that uses red or yellow fonts? Exactly. So, as a general rule, don't use more than two different fonts in a presentation. And stick to white or black fonts. There is a reason why publishers stick to these colors. They are easier on the eyes to read.

F. Use high quality images.

People today are use to great graphics on their high-definition televisions, computers and tablets. The high-tech world has raised the bar on what is acceptable in the world of graphic arts. So, don't ever use low quality, blurry or pixilated images in your presentation. There's no need to. You can find free, high-resolution, public domain photographs at:

- FreeImages.com
- Wikimedia.org

For a few dollars you can find excellent photographs of Israel, archaeological sites, open Bibles, people, etc. at:

- Dreamstime.com
- DepositPhotos.com
- BiblePlaces.com
- Istock.com

G. Whenever possible, avoid stretching out an image in a way that the original proportions are skewed.

Many a presenter has thought, "This photograph is too narrow. I'll just stretch it out a bit. There!" I encourage you to avoid doing this if it makes the photograph look awkward, as is almost always the case with pictures of people.

78. Set up a good filing system for illustrations and other interesting information.

"The words of wise men are like goads,
and masters of these collections are like
well-driven nails." (Ecc. 12:11)

If you are going to be teaching on a consistent basis, I strongly suggest that you set up two filing systems for illustrations, one on your computer and the other in a filing cabinet.

A. Illustrations on your computer

Putting illustrations on your computer will obviously make retrieving them much easier than looking through books, searching online, etc. Here's how I do it. In my "Documents" folder I created a folder called "Bible Studies." Then in that folder I have created subfolders:

- Old Testament Books
- New Testament Books
- Topical Messages
- Illustrations
- Easter Messages
- Christmas Messages
- Etc.

This "Illustrations" folder is where I keep all of my illustrations. When I find a good story, quote, or think of a good illustration on "forgiveness" or "lying," I type it into a new blank document (or an existing one if I've already found illustrations on that topic). Then I save the document with the appropriate title "Forgiveness" or "Lying." When I find another illustration on the same topic, I place it in the same document separated by a line.

Now, a year later when I need an illustration on forgiveness or lying, I open up my "Illustrations" folder and there are my illustrations, in alphabetical order, long after I have forgotten about them.

Above the lengthier illustrations I put a one-sentence summary so that I can quickly scroll through the illustrations months later without having to spend time reading each one. This may sound time consuming, but doing this—being organized—has actually *saved* me lots of time when the need for a particular illustration comes up.

B. Illustrations in your filing cabinet

In addition to using your computer, I also suggest that you create files in a filing cabinet for articles, photocopies and other interesting information you come across throughout the year.

Before I throw away a copy of a magazine, I tear out any of the articles that struck me as good illustrative material. I'll quickly write a big one or two-word summary on the page with a black Sharpie and save them for future use. Consider doing this as well.

CONCLUSION

We have covered a lot of ground in this book. I hope you have found the suggestions, ideas, exhortations and words of encouragement to be helpful in your desire to grow as a teacher. Obviously a lot more could be said about this important topic. With that in mind, I have included a list of recommended resources at the end of the book. Before we part ways, I'd like to pray for you.

> Father in Heaven, Creator of galaxies too numerous to count, thank You for Your Word. Thank You for life, abundant life, and the opportunity to not only know You now and throughout eternity but to make You known to others through the preaching of Your Word. What a blessing! And Father, I thank You for the person holding this book. You created him. You love him. You've got great plans for him. I pray Lord that You will take the words he has read and pondered in these pages and sanctify them. I

pray that by Your Spirit, You will help him to hold on to, remember, and implement what is good and pleasing in Your sight. And I pray You will blow away anything that would hinder him from becoming the kind of teacher You desire to make him. You've seen the things he's underlined in this book; You know the sections where his heart was stirred by the Holy Spirit. Continue to work in those areas that he might continue to grow and mature as a faithful, fruitful proclaimer of Your truth. I don't know where You are leading the reader or where You have him, but wherever he goes as he follows You, I pray God that You will bless him and strengthen him. Help him to live a godly life, fight a good fight, walk circumspectly around Satan's snares, keep his hand to the plow and his eyes on Jesus. So God, draw near to him. Bless his quiet time in Your Word. May Your Spirit daily instruct and encourage him, nourish his soul and cause love for You, people and the truth to run over. And I pray all these things in the name above all other names—the name of our great God and Savior, Jesus. Amen.

I welcome your thoughts...

I would love to hear your feedback, as well as your thoughts and ideas for improving future printings.

Email me at: **info@alwaysbeready.com**

APPENDIX

SERMON EVALUATION CHECK LIST

Many years ago I taught a course on preaching at Calvary Chapel Vista's School of Ministry. I called the class "Homiletics" as any good seminary would do. The first time we offered it, hardly anyone signed up. The name of the class surely confused or intimidated people, even though the course catalog described what the class entailed. The second and subsequent times we offered the class, we called it "The Preaching Lab" and had a much bigger enrollment.

In the class we always spent the last several weeks having the students prepare messages and teach them to their classmates. My desire was to give them instruction on preaching and some actual experience doing so. When the student was done teaching, we would offer encouraging feedback and constructive advice.

To help those who listened to the sermons keep track of their thoughts and comments, I prepared a list of questions for them to refer to while the teaching was going on. I include those questions here—not so you can grade your pastor as he teaches—but so that you might, should you decide to, go back over any of your own teachings to look for areas to improve. Another possible use for these questions would be to put them in the hands of a person you want to evaluate your teaching.

1. Was there an opening prayer?
2. Was the introduction interesting, short, clear?
3. Did the teacher ask you to open up the Word and read along?
4. Was the text broken down and explained clearly?
5. Were the who, what, why, where, how, when questions answered?
6. Did the message flow smoothly?
7. Was there good eye contact?
8. Were the illustrations clear? Necessary? Beneficial?
9. Was the message Biblically sound? Did you see any verses or passages used incorrectly?
10. Did the teacher seem as if he really believed what he was saying?
11. Did he speak directly to the listeners, using the word "you"?
12. Do you think God was glorified?
13. Was there a challenge to believe or obey the Word?
14. Were ideas given about how the passage could apply to the listeners?

15. Was the grace of God or the empowering of the Holy Spirit mentioned along with commands to obey?
16. Were the Biblical truths brought into the present or did they linger in the past?
17. Did the message point people to Jesus?
18. Was the message convincing or persuasive?
19. Did the message edify, comfort, exhort (1 Cor. 14:3)?
20. Was the gospel preached?
21. Was there a strong conclusion?
22. Should the sermon have been shorter or longer?
23. Did it appear as though the teacher was well prepared?
24. Was there any distracting body language?
25. What did you like about the message and or delivery?
26. What else might you suggest to help the person improve?

Recommended RESOURCES

Alphabetically Listed by Title

Anointed Expository Preaching
Stephen Olford and David Olford

Between Two Worlds
John Stott

Biblical Preaching
Haddon Robinson

Christ-Centered Preaching
Bryan Chapell

**Deep Preaching: Creating Sermons that
Go Beyond the Superficial**
J. Kent Edwards

He Is Not Silent: Preaching in a Postmodern World
Albert Mohler

Jottings and Hints for Lay Preachers
F. B. Myer

Lectures on Preaching
Alistair Begg
(Download audio at: http://www.truthforlife.org/
resources/?topic=preaching)

Lectures to My Students
Charles Spurgeon

Preach the Word
Leland Ryken and Todd Wilson (eds.)

Preach the Word Conference DVDs
(Conference videos available at harvest.org/ptw)

Preaching
G. Campbell Morgan

Preaching & Preachers
Martyn Lloyd-Jones

Preaching for God's Glory
Alistair Begg

Rediscovering Expository Preaching
John MacArthur and The Master's
Seminary Faculty

The Elements of Preaching
Warren Wiersbe and David Wiersbe

The Reformed Pastor
Richard Baxter

The Supremacy of God in Preaching
John Piper

About the author...

CHARLIE H. CAMPBELL

Charlie Campbell is the Director of the Always Be Ready Apologetics Ministry, an ordained pastor, author, and a popular guest teacher at

churches around North America, speaking regularly on a wide variety of issues related to the Christian faith. His books and DVDs have been endorsed by:

- Charles Colson
- Norman Geisler
- Chuck Smith
- Ed Hindson
- Nancy Leigh DeMoss

Prior to his current role, he served as the Director of the School of Ministry at Calvary Chapel in Vista, California, where he taught courses on systematic theology, apologetics, world religions, cults, eschatology, hermeneutics, homiletics and evangelism (1997–2006). He resides in southern California with his wife and five children.

Website: AlwaysBeReady.com
Email: info@alwaysbeready.com
Twitter: @CharlieABReady
Instagram: Charlie_H_Campbell

Check out Charlie Campbell's
Other Books and DVDs:

Available at AlwaysBeReady.com

- *Evidence for God*
- *Answers to Atheists' Attacks on Jesus*
- *Scrolls & Stones: Compelling Evidence the Bible Can Be Trusted*
- *Archaeological Evidence for the Bible*
- *Evidence for the Bible: Ten Reasons to Trust the Scriptures*
- *One Minute Answers to Skeptics' Top Forty Questions*
- *If God is Loving, Why is there Evil and Suffering?*
- *Homosexuality & the Bible: Answering Objections to the Biblical View*
- *Answers to the Tough Questions About Hell*
- *Answering the Cults' Attacks on Jesus' Deity*
- *The Case for the Resurrection*
- *All Roads Do Not Lead to God*
- *Answers to Skeptics' Top Ten Questions*
- *Reaching the Lost*
- *Overcoming the Fear of Evangelism*
- *The End Times & Beyond: Ten Upcoming Events in Bible Prophecy*
- *The Case for a Pretribulational Rapture*
- *The Second Coming, Preterism, & the Book of Revelation*
- *Islam*
- *Jehovah's Witnesses*
- *Mormonism*
- *Roman Catholicism*
- *New Age Spirituality*
- *Judaism*
- *Hinduism*
- *Buddhism*

Made in the USA
San Bernardino, CA
26 March 2017